TWENTIETH CENTURY VIEWS

The aim of this series is to present the best in contemporary critical opinion on major authors, providing a twentieth century perspective on their changing status in an era of profound revaluation.

Maynard Mack, *Series Editor*
Yale University

THURBER

"All Right, Have It Your Way—
You Heard a Seal Bark!"

THURBER

A COLLECTION OF CRITICAL ESSAYS

Edited by

Charles S. Holmes

Prentice-Hall, Inc. *Englewood Cliffs, N.J.*

A SPECTRUM BOOK

Library of Congress Cataloging in Publication Data

HOLMES, CHARLES SHIVELEY, comp.
    Thurber: a collection of critical essays.

    (Twentieth century views) (A Spectrum Book)
    Bibliography: p.
    1. Thurber, James, 1894–1961. I. Title.
PS3539.H94Z72   818'.5'209   74–9563
ISBN 0–13–920793–7
ISBN 0–13–920785–6 (pbk.)

10   9   8   7   6   5   4   3   2   1

PRENTICE-HALL INTERNATIONAL, INC. (*London*)
PRENTICE-HALL OF AUSTRALIA, PTY. LTD. (*Sydney*)
PRENTICE-HALL OF CANADA, LTD. (*Toronto*)
PRENTICE-HALL OF INDIA PRIVATE LIMITED (*New Delhi*)
PRENTICE-HALL OF JAPAN, INC. (*Tokyo*)

Acknowledgments

Quotations from *My Life and Hard Times* by James Thurber are used by kind permission of Mrs. James Thurber and Hamish Hamilton Ltd. Copyright © 1933, 1961 by James Thurber. *My Life and Hard Times* is published by Harper & Row, New York.

Quotations from *Let Your Mind Alone* by James Thurber are used by kind permission of Mrs. James Thurber and Hamish Hamilton Ltd. Copyright © 1937 by James Thurber. Copyright © 1965 by Helen W. Thurber and Rosemary Thurber Sauers. *Let Your Mind Alone* was published by Harper & Row, New York.

Quotations from "The Rose and the Weed," in *Further Fables for Our Time* by James Thurber, are used by kind permission of Mrs. James Thurber. *Further Fables for Our Time* is published by Simon and Schuster, Inc.

Permission to reprint the following has been granted by Harcourt Brace Jovanovich, Inc. and Faber and Faber Ltd:

Three lines from "The Love Song of J. Alfred Prufrock," by T. S. Eliot from *Collected Poems 1909–1962*. These appear on page 38 of the present volume.

Four lines from "The Waste Land," by T. S. Eliot from *Collected Poems 1909–1962*. These appear on page 41 of the present volume.

The frontispiece is used by the kind permission of Mrs. James Thurber and Hamish Hamilton Ltd. Copyright © 1932, 1960 by James Thurber. From *The Seal in the Bedroom* by James Thurber, published by Harper & Row, New York. Copyright © 1963 by Hamish Hamilton, London. From *Vintage Thurber* by James Thurber. It was originally printed in *The New Yorker*.

Contents

I. Traditions

II. The Individual Talent: Early and Middle Years

III.   The Later Years

IV. Snapshots

Introduction

by Charles S. Holmes

It is by now a truism to say that James Thurber is the greatest American humorist since Mark Twain. His imagination was tuned to the discords of the twentieth century with preternatural accuracy. In his stories, essays, and drawings we find comic images of our public and private apprehensions: the character of Walter Mitty, as *Time* magazine once said, stands with Leopold Bloom and Hans Castorp as an archetype of modern man. Malcolm Cowley called his prose style one of the best in modern literature, and *The Times Literary Supplement* observed that almost alone among living American writers, he was as "comprehensible and lovable to the European mind as . . . to the mind of his countrymen." [1] His first book, *Is Sex Necessary?*, written in collaboration with his friend E. B. White, was a best seller, and throughout his long career he enjoyed a steadily increasing popularity with high and middlebrow readers. He has been translated into nearly every European language, and the British admiration of him is little short of idolatrous.

Perhaps this very popularity is the reason that there is as yet only a small body of criticism of his work. Most of what there is appears in reviews and occasional brief essays. We feel that popular writers, especially popular humorists, do not need or warrant the same kind of critical attention we give to our "serious" writers. Secretly we feel that the comic view of life is somehow superficial or, if not superficial, simply beyond rational discussion. To write about a humorist is either to show one's self a pedant or to abandon intellectual and aesthetic standards altogether. Then too, although his talent is clearly major, Thurber worked almost exclusively in the minor forms. He wrote no novels, only a few poems, and of his two ventures into the theater, one was a collaboration with Elliott Nugent and the other an adaptation of his own already published

[1] *Friday*, October 10, 1952, p. 658.

1

work. For the most part, he limited himself to the very short *New Yorker* story and the humorous autobiographical sketch, and these look slight, even collected in book form, when compared to the output of, say, F. Scott Fitzgerald, whose creative gifts were surely no greater than Thurber's. Nevertheless, although there has not yet been the systematic and detailed study of Thurber that there has been of Fitzgerald, the selections collected here show—with a few interesting exceptions—a common recognition of his originality and importance as an interpreter of modern life, and at least the beginnings of an effort to give serious critical consideration to his themes and artistic method.

II

Thurber was born and raised in Columbus, Ohio, and although he found his artistic identity on *The New Yorker* and lived most of his life in New York and Connecticut, the taproot of his imagination led back to his early years in Ohio. "I have always waved banners and blown horns for Good Old Columbus Town . . . and such readers as I have collected over the years are all aware of where I was born and brought up, and they know that half my books could not have been written if it had not been for the city of my birth," he announced in 1959, lapsing easily into the rhetoric of small-town boosterism. On the other hand, it is but one of the paradoxes of his complex nature that he was a Columbus newspaperman who also read Joyce, worshiped Henry James, and wrote highly sophisticated and bookish humor. He was a combination of old-fashioned Midwestern values and international intellectual culture, and it is the tension between these forces which underlies much of his humor and at least some of the pathos in his work. Setting this point in the context of literary history, John Seelye sees Thurber as uniting two primary impulses in American humor—the urbane and civilized comedy of Washington Irving, Stephen Leacock, and E. B. White, and the wild uninhibited spirit of Twain and the tall-tale tellers of the Southwestern frontier.

At the age of seven, Thurber suffered the injury which led to his total blindness some forty years later. Playing cowboys and Indians with his brothers, he was shot in the left eye by an arrow. His handicap kept him out of the sports enjoyed by other boys, and, in compensation, he developed his already rich fantasy life, writing stories, drawing pictures, and acting out playlets for his family and friends. He was passionately devoted to dime novels, comic strips, theatrical melodramas, and the movies. When he began to write, he drew heavily upon such popular sources. He particularly valued those comic strips which, like Cliff Sterrett's "Polly and Her Pals" or Clare Briggs's "When a Feller Needs a Friend," focussed on the everyday domestic scene. But, as John Seelye points out, he was equally devoted to strips like "The Toonerville Trolley," which treated small-town life in terms of comic mayhem and chaos. And, although he had little to say about it, the Keystone Cops brand of film comedy must also lie behind the broad farce and slam-bang vaudeville of *My Life and Hard Times.*

The popular arts were his first love, but at Ohio State University he encountered Henry James in a course given by Professor Joseph Russell Taylor, one of the university's great teachers, and he was never quite the same thereafter. James quickly became one of the enduring passions of Thurber's life, a permanent touchstone of artistic and moral value. *The Ambassadors* was his favorite book, and when he first went to Europe, in 1918, as a code clerk with the U.S. Embassy in Paris, he saw the whole experience through Jamesian eyes. Edward Stone, in "Thurber's Four Pieces," shows how consistently Thurber drew upon, imitated, parodied, and referred to James throughout his career. Late in life he expressed some doubt about James's relevance to modern problems, but this was only a temporary apostasy. His literary taste, shaped by his reading at Ohio State and by Taylor, ran to the genteel, the perfectly ordered, and the highly polished, as opposed to what he called "the sprawling chunk of life." In a letter to his daughter, he listed the writers who had "interested, inspired, or excited" him. Among them were Willa Cather, Evelyn Waugh, Nathanael West, Clarence Day, Ernest Hemingway, and E. B. White. His favorite book by a living author was *The Great Gatsby.* In the interview with Plimpton and Steele, he quoted Fitzgerald's remark to Thomas Wolfe: "You're a putter-inner and I'm a taker-outer," and it is obvious that he preferred the taker-outers. His own work was done slowly and with scrupulous care. Writing for him was mostly a matter of rewriting, he said to Plimpton and Steele. He rewrote "The Secret Life of Walter Mitty" fifteen times, and it took him eight weeks to do it.

Thurber's arrival on the staff of *The New Yorker* was a turning point in his life and in that of the magazine as well. In 1927, *The New Yorker* was a hopeful but shaky venture, and Thurber was an obscure newspaperman with literary ambitions. Under the congenial influence of White and the demanding editorial eye of Harold Ross, Thurber purged himself of a tendency to overwrite and quickly developed the easy, informal, flexible style which—along with White's—made *The New Yorker* famous. Thurber acknowledged his indebtedness to White on many occasions. "Until I learned discipline in writing from studying Andy White's stuff, I was a careless, nervous, headlong writer, trailing the phrases and rhythms of Henry James, Hergesheimer, Henley, and my favorite English teacher at Ohio State, Joe Taylor," he said in a letter to Frank Gibney in 1956. Ross's insistence on clarity and accuracy was another salutary discipline; "it kept us from getting sloppy," Thurber told Plimpton and Steele.

His first major assignment was "The Talk of the Town," the department of miscellaneous verbal snapshots of the city scene which, with White's "Notes and Comment," set the tone of the magazine. Thurber was editor, reporter, and rewrite man for "Talk" from 1929 to 1935. Robert M. Coates, one of his close associates on the magazine, recalls that he had precisely the talents called for: the reportorial eye, the imagination to see the unusual and the comic in the commonplace, and an unassuming but expressive style.

If Thurber's early *New Yorker* experience was first of all a process of artistic discipline, it was also, as John Seelye observes, a time of liberation. His creative talent flowered in the years after he joined the magazine. *Is Sex Necessary?* (1929), *The Owl in the Attic* (1931), *The Seal in the Bedroom* (1932), *My Life and Hard Times* (1933), and *The Middle-Aged Man on the Flying Trapeze* (1935) established him as a writer and cartoonist of rare originality. Here were the subjects, characters, and themes which identified his work up to the period of his blindness: the domestic scene and the trivia which somehow explode into major conflicts; the timid daydreamy men and the aggressive practical women; the view of marriage as a state of undeclared war; the celebration of the natural, the individual, the eccentric as against conventions, formulas, and systems of all kinds; and above all, the constant and surprising interplay of reality and fantasy.

Whether Thurber made *The New Yorker* or *The New Yorker* made Thurber is a question to which the answer must be yes on both counts. Neither would have flourished so vigorously without the other. Richard Luckett, in a recent essay-review in *The Spectator*, argues that the genteel standards and the tight formal requirements of the magazine may have inhibited Thurber's growth as a writer.[2] It is true that Thurber sometimes confessed that years of

2 "Review of Books," *The Spectator*, May 19, 1973, pp. 618–19.

writing *New Yorker* pieces made everything he started—play, novel, or whatever—turn out to be a six- or seven-page "casual." And in later years he complained that the magazine had become too smooth and feminized and was falling into "a tulle and taffeta rut." But it is doubtful that Thurber was a frustrated Rabelais or Cervantes. The polite inhibitions of *The New Yorker* reflected his own, and the formal limitations of the magazine were exactly what he needed to make the most of his idiosyncratic talent.

III

Thurber was received enthusiastically from the first, but it was the English who made the first real effort to see him as something more than a popular entertainer. David Garnett, reviewing *Let Your Mind Alone* in *The New Statesman* in 1937, called Thurber "the most original and humorous writer living," and went on to point out that much of his humor was not reassuring, but "savage," and that some of his stories, such as "The Wood Duck," are not humorous at all, but serious fiction of a high order. As early as 1931, Paul Nash, the English painter and critic, called attention to Thurber in an essay called "American Humorous Draughtsmen" in *The Week-End Review*.[3] Praising the artists of *The New Yorker*, he observed that Soglow and Thurber were "draughtsmen of the single line, using it as a child might," in the manner of Matisse. By 1949, *The Times Literary Supplement* could say without self-consciousness that Thurber had become an institution, and from now on would have to be reviewed like one. Generally speaking, British readers find something authentically American in Thurber's voice as well as in his subject matter. They like the vein of fantasy in his work, and they are more responsive than American readers to the dark side of his imagination, to the pessimism and the sense of disaster which give Thurber's world its special atmosphere. At the same time, they admire his "civilized" qualities—the craftsmanship and the classic economy of style. Thurber reciprocated. He often said that the English were his best and most discriminating audience, and that whenever he visited London, which was often, he felt as though he were coming home.

The first American recognition of Thurber's importance as an interpreter of modern life was Peter De Vries's 1943 essay in *Poetry*, "James Thurber: The Comic Prufrock." De Vries argues that Thurber's true affinity is with the Symbolist poets rather than with the

[3] August 8, 1931, pp. 163–64.

humorists. Like them, he celebrates the subjective vision, and in his work there are the same quick shifts from outer to inner experience, the same transformations of reality into dream and fantasy that we find in T. S. Eliot. When Barney Haller, the handyman with the heavy German accent, announces "Bimeby I go hunt grotches in de voods," the everyday scene is suddenly transformed into a nightmare vision of "ugly little creatures, about the size of whippoorwills, only covered with blood and honey and the scraping of church bells," and of Barney presiding over unspeakable ceremonies. The strange world opened up by Della's garbling of familiar words and phrases (" 'They are here with the reeves' ") is an exciting alternative to the world of commonplace reality, as are the visions revealed to Thurber when he breaks his glasses ("I saw a gay old lady with a parasol walk right through the side of a truck."). For him, as for the Symbolists, the life of fantasy is superior to the life of reality. In De Vries's fine phrase, Thurber is the "jester in Axel's Castle," giving us a comic version of the areas of experience explored by the poets of the Symbolist tradition. His timid, neurotic protagonists are the direct descendants of Eliot's J. Alfred Prufrock—and, as Edward Stone suggests, of Henry James's "poor sensitive gentlemen."

Thurber's great subject is the predicament of man in a baffling and alien world. Cut off from the simpler, stabler order of the past, which Thurber's nostalgic pieces constantly evoke, modern man leads a precarious existence. Trapped in a world of machines and gadgets which challenge his competence and threaten his sanity, a world of large organizations and mass-mindedness which threatens his individuality, and—most painfully—a world of aggressive women who threaten his masculine identity, he is forced to go underground, so to speak, and to fight back in small, secret ways. Unlike Prufrock, Thurber's protagonists do resist, finding in daydream and fantasy the means to reshape outer defeat into inner victory, as Walter Mitty does. Occasionally, the victory is unequivocal, like that of the husband in "The Unicorn in the Garden" and of Mr. Martin in "The Catbird Seat," but open triumph is not the usual destiny of the Thurber male.

As Walter Blair and Norris Yates point out, Thurber's Little Man has a good deal in common with the antiheroes of twentieth-century fiction. Thurber did not invent this character for American humor—Benchley did that, following the model of Stephen Leacock—but he enlarged it, gave it a new psychological dimension, and made it into a highly effective dramatic persona. The mocking self-portrait in the preface to *My Life and Hard Times* invites the reader to see the author as one of his own apprehensive, maladjusted, anxiety-ridden characters; and, although there is a good deal of Thurber in the figure, it is Thurber with the Prufrockian side of his character played up and the strength and aggressiveness left out. Walter Mitty is Thurber, but so is the man equal to all occasions, the late-night party entertainer, and the intimidating opponent in argument (the louder and more illogical the better) described by Peter De Vries in "Thurber the Talker." Wolcott Gibbs, speaking of the differences between Thurber's fantasy image of himself and his "real" self, observed that in any contest of personalities involving Thurber, "everybody else would be well advised to take to the hills."

The Little Man is the most famous of Thurber's personae, but as Yates points out, it is not the only one. Throughout his career he wrote as a reporter, social historian, memoirist, and biographer, in addition to his work as a humorist; and, in these roles, he customarily speaks in the voice of the educated and enlightened observer of the human scene. As he became more and more concerned over what was happening to American life in the 1940s and 1950s, the identity of the Little Man no longer served his needs, and he adopted instead the traditional role of the social critic and satirist, speaking out as rational man and public-spirited citizen against the fanaticisms and vulgarities of the day. These two personae—one, the helpless Little Man, the other the aggressive reformer and man of liberal principles—embody two conflicting views of life; and, as Yates points out, Thurber never harmonized or reconciled them. When he tried, in the character of Tommy Turner, in *The Male Animal,* the result was unconvincing.

IV

Thurber's drawings, those strange, childlike scrawls blending the worlds of reality and dream, are the purest expression of his imagination, but they are so difficult to describe and to relate to the traditions of art that critical comment on them is thin indeed. Thurber always deprecated them because they came easily, whereas his writing came hard. He boasted that he had never taken longer than three minutes on any drawing, and he used to dash them off at parties and give them to friends with reckless prodigality. He disliked being identified as " 'Thurber, the bird who draws.' " "I'm not an artist, I'm a painstaking writer who doodles for relaxation," he said to Arthur Millier of the *Los Angeles Times* in 1939. Nevertheless, he has always been as widely known for his drawings as for his prose. Critics were fascinated by the similarity of his radical simplification of form to the deliberate primitivism of such modern masters as Picasso and Matisse. Throughout his career he was featured in important gallery shows: in 1934, there was a one-man show at the Valentine Gallery in New York; the Museum of Modern Art included him in its show of Dada, surrealism, and fantastic art in 1936; and in 1937, the Storran Gallery in London mounted a highly successful one-man exhibition which established him as a British favorite.

When Thurber and White showed the drawings for *Is Sex Necessary?* to the editors of Harper and Brothers, there was a silence, after which one of them asked uneasily, "I gather these are a rough idea of the kind of illustrations you want some artist to do?" "These are the drawings that go into the book," said White firmly, and Thurber's public career as an artist was under way. There is always an element of shock in Thurber's drastic reduction of familiar forms. Ronald Searle, the English artist, described his style as "a form of Neolithic shorthand"; Lisle Bell, reviewing *The Seal in the Bedroom,* suggested that Thurber might have been influenced by what he had seen in Egyptian tombs and abandoned telephone booths.

In any case, Thurber's drawings are not representations of things as they are, but presentations of things as they appear in the imagination. The effect of their reductiveness is comic, satiric, and pathetic. As Dorothy Parker observes, Thurber's people have "the outer semblance of unbaked cookies." In the total absence of the details and proportions which give the human form individuality, beauty, and nobility there is both pity and misanthropy. Thurber often said that he simply could not draw good-looking men and women, implying (not very convincingly) that the trouble was technical rather than philosophical. Kenneth MacLean has suggested that the formlessness of Thurber's drawings is the expression of his sense of the formlessness of life itself. The essence of the comic in a Thurber story is the disruption of order. In his drawings, he presents us with a world in which Aristotelian forms have been dissolved and replaced by the free play of "imaginative and symbolic life." [4] W. H. Auden, in "The Icon and the Portrait," sets Thurber

---

4 "The Imagination of James Thurber," *The Canadian Forum* 33 (December, 1953): 200.

in the long tradition of Western symbolic art and the comic branch of it which stems from Edward Lear. From this vantage point, we see Thurber's reductive style as a sign of the sensitive artist's repudiation of the outer world, now appropriated by purely materialistic forces, and his turning inward to one of his own making.

The vein of fantasy is even stronger in the drawings than in the stories. Most of them present scenes that, as Dorothy Parker points out, are mysterious and inexplicable. They haunt the imagination because they seem to have popped up from the unconscious or to have been recalled from dreams. The famous "All right, have it your way, you heard a seal bark" simply resists logical explanation. The man and the woman are there all right, and so is the seal. There is no indication that the seal is any less "real" than the man and the woman; but how he got there, and what his presence means, we shall never know.

When asked to explain his drawings, Thurber usually stressed their spontaneous origin, and the consequent impossibility of finding any rational meaning in them. He once put them into three categories: 1) those which came from the unconscious, 2) those which were the result of accident, and 3) those which were planned or thought up.[5] The "Seal" is a classic example of the happy result of what aestheticians call the Creative Accident. Thurber started out to do a seal on a rock, but as he drew, the rock looked like the head of a bed, and so he simply followed out the logic of this new possibility and gave the woman her immortal line to speak. Making due allowance for some leg-pulling, it is no doubt true that most of Thurber's drawings were as surprising to him as to his audience, and that his best ones, such as "That's my first wife up there . . ." and "What Have You Done With Dr. Millmoss?," came into being in just such a way.

V

The publication of *The Thurber Carnival* in 1945 excited both popular and critical attention. Like a retrospective art show, this selection of his best prose and drawings over a fifteen-year period demonstrated his stature and significance in a way that the separate *New Yorker* pieces, and even such fine collections as *The Middle-Aged Man on the Flying Trapeze*, had never quite done. Dan Norton spoke for critics and general readers alike when he said, "The

[5] "The Lady on the Bookcase," *The Beast in Me and Other Animals* (New York: Harcourt, Brace and Co., 1948).

man, or at least his work, is here to stay. We can no longer be content simply to laugh at what he produces; we must make a deter-
mined effort to understand him as man and artist." [6] Among the
many perceptive assessments of Thurber's achievement occasioned
by the *Carnival,* the most illuminating is Malcolm Cowley's "James
Thurber's Dream Book," which says so much in its brief compass
that one wishes that Cowley had written the full-dress critical study
of Thurber he planned but never quite got around to in the 1950s.
Cowley emphasizes, as no one had before, the dark strain in Thurber, the concentration on violence, murder, madness, nightmare,
and hallucination. Most of the pieces in question are funny, but
the humor is cruel and sadistic, like that in "The Cane in the Corridor," surely one of Thurber's masterpieces.

Beginning with Cowley's essay, one can identify two ways of looking at Thurber: one, the "dark," psychological view, emphasizing
the neurotic and unsettling elements in his work; the other the
"light," rational view, emphasizing its aesthetic and humanistic
qualities. The humanistic view sees Thurber as the defender of the
individual in an age of mass culture, the champion of imagination
over the logic-and-formula-ridden mind, the enemy of political fanaticism, whether of the Right or Left. This is the Thurber of *My
Life and Hard Times, Let Your Mind Alone, The Male Animal,
Fables for Our Time, The Last Flower* (if read optimistically, as
E. B. White does), *The White Deer,* and perhaps *The Thurber
Album.* It is also the Thurber who refused to despair when he lost
his sight in middle age, and who, though embittered by what
seemed to him the disappearance of all the old standards and de-
cencies after World War II, could still say, "let's not look back in
anger, or forward in fear, but around in awareness."

Robert Elias argues persuasively for the optimistic view. His
"James Thurber: the Primitive, the Innocent, and the Individual,"
emphasizes the consistency of Thurber's concern with discovering
and celebrating values to live by in the modern world. Elias sees
Thurber's career as a steady growth in moral perception and artistic mastery, particularly in the years following "The Secret Life
of Walter Mitty" and *Fables for Our Time.* He does not ignore the
melancholy which colors Thurber's work, but he insists on a basic
"humanistic affirmation" which holds it all together and makes it
a valuable criticism of life.

The darker view focuses on Thurber as a man writing to exorcise
a deep inner uncertainty, to come to terms with fears and resent-

[6] *The New York Times Book Review,* February 4, 1945, p. 1.

ments which threatened his psychic balance. Images of these neurotic forces are everywhere in his work—in the Preface to *My Life and Hard Times,* in the discords of *The Middle-Aged Man on the Flying Trapeze,* in the strange drawings, in Walter Mitty's escapism, in stories such as "The Whippoorwill," in *Further Fables for Our Time,* and in the compulsive wordplay of the late pieces. Honor Tracy, the Irish novelist and Thurber admirer, observes, "I know of no comic writer, indeed of hardly any writer at all, who more deftly awakens unease, anxiety and dread in the heart than Thurber." [7] And John Updike speaks eloquently of the "cosmic background of gathering dark" against which Thurber's humor plays.

VI

In the spring of 1940, Thurber began to lose the sight in his remaining good eye. After 1941, he could no longer read or see the keys well enough to work at the typewriter. The shock of having to find a whole new way of making contact with the world brought on what he later called "a five-year nervous crack-up," but during it he taught himself to compose in longhand at first, writing with a soft pencil on yellow paper in a barely decipherable scrawl, and later, when he could no longer see at all, by dictation. The effect of blindness on Thurber's style and subject matter was profound. First of all, it drove him inward and backward to the world of childhood fantasy. The fairy tales—*Many Moons* (1943), *The Great Quillow* (1944), *The White Deer* (1945), *The Thirteen Clocks* (1950)—are not only escapes from a painful present reality into a world of romance and make-believe; they are also affirmations of certain values which had come to have a special importance for him. All of them, as Richard Tobias points out, tell the story of a blighted land, of the failure of the king's advisers—scientists and men of power—to remedy the situation, and of the lifting of the spell by the lowly regarded court jester, toymaker, poet, or minstrel, in short, by the man of creative imagination.

Blindness also intensified Thurber's lifelong preoccupation with language. Cut off from the visible world, he became obsessed with words as things in themselves. The grounds of his comedy shift from the play of character and situation to that of verbal encounter, repartee, and word gamesmanship. Beginning with *The White Deer,* he develops a style very different from the understated economy of

7 "The Claw of the Sea Puss," *The Listener* 47 (May 10, 1951): 760.

his earlier prose. This new style is elaborate and decorative, full of puns, garbles, coinages, and literary allusions. Reviewing *Further Fables for Our Time*, Malcolm Cowley made the point that, since Thurber's blindness, all the sound effects in his prose had become intensified, "as if one sense had been developed at the cost of another." Thurber's recent work, he added, presents us with "a completely verbalized universe."

Two new forms characterize this later period: the conversation piece, a party scene in which the guests try to hoax and intimidate one another with bravura displays of wit, dictionary lore, puns, and literary allusions; and the word-game piece, usually an insomniac monologue in which Thurber plays desperately with the sound and structure of words, taking them apart, spelling them backward, and recombining them into strange, comic, and unsettling new combinations. Here is his anatomy of the word "music," in "Conversation Piece: Connecticut":

> "The word is icsum and mucsi," I said. "It is also musci and scumi. If you say 'sicum!' your dog starts barking at nothing, and if you say 'sucim,' the pigs in the barnyard start squealing and grunting. 'Muics' is the cat's miaow. Say 'miscu' and your fingers are fungers. Say 'umsci' and the Russians are upon you. As for mucis—my God, are you ready for another drink already?"

A growing pessimism and misanthropy accompany the changes in the form and subject matter of Thurber's later work. The bitter humor of *Further Fables for Our Time* signalizes the change in his view of life: "Open most heads and you will find nothing shining, not even a mind," runs the moral of "The Truth About Toads." As it did for the older Mark Twain, Thurber's inner melancholy fed a sense of daily outrage at the public scene. He saw the postwar world as a time of intellectual and moral confusion. "I think there's been a fall-out of powdered fruitcake—everyone's going nuts," he remarked in an interview. In the era of the Bomb and McCarthyism, he saw man as less the victim of a too-complex society and more a creature given over to folly and self-destruction. Earlier, in *Fables for Our Time* and *The Male Animal* (1940), he had spoken out against totalitarianism abroad and fascism at home, but, generally, he had always argued that the humorist should stay out of the political arena and concentrate on the private dilemmas of the individual person. Now, as the threat to freedom of thought mounted in the late 1940s and the 1950s, his work became increasingly political, as Yates, Weales, and Morsberger point out, and he began to argue for the socially redemptive value of humor.

The theme of all of Thurber's later work is decline—of form, style, good sense, "human stature, hope, humor." The spirit of the late pieces is satiric rather than humorous: "anger," he observed in the foreword to *Lanterns and Lances,* has become "one of the necessary virtues." The center of his concern became the state of the language, which for him, as for Ezra Pound and George Orwell, was the index to the state of a culture. The outrages perpetrated by politicians, administrators, and psychologists against the language prompted him to bend Goldsmith to the occasion: " 'Ill fares the land, to galloping fears a prey, where gobbledygook accumulates, and words decay.' " Even worse was the deliberate vulgarization of speech in the mass media. Everywhere he looked, he saw the decay of forms and standards. In these late essays on the state of culture in the modern world, Thurber is defending the old virtues against the new barbarism, building walls, as Paul Jennings observes, against chaos. Earlier in his life, Thurber celebrated disorder, illogic, and confusion, feeling that these were desirable counterbalances in a society overcommitted to science and efficiency. Later, as history changed the world he grew up in, and his own view of life changed, he looked for stability and continuity, and championed those qualities which hold a society together.

The later Thurber, like the later Henry James, appeals chiefly to the special taste of a loyal coterie. Gerald Weales speaks of the hard moral wisdom and imaginative vitality of *Further Fables for Our Time* (1956), but many readers find the gloomy world view and obsessive verbal play of *Lanterns and Lances* (1961) and the posthumous *Credos and Curios* sterile, precious, and even tedious. John Mortimer objects to the self-consciously literary quality of the later Thurber, although he praises the insomniac pieces as dramatizing the "two great American terrors, that of sleeplessness and of large, predatory and highly sexed women." John Updike complains that too often "logomachic tricks are asked to pass for wit and implausible pun-swapping for human conversation." Worse yet, the diatribes against the decadence of contemporary culture are so indiscriminate as to be pointless: by the end of the 1950s, in Updike's harsh judgment, Thurber had simply become "one more indignant senior citizen penning complaints about the universal decay of virtue." Jesse Bier takes Updike's point even farther. The misanthropy and ingrown word-play of the last years represents "a retreat from humor" characteristic of the whole generation of writers who came on the scene after World War II. In this view, Thurber's career is striking evidence of "the decline and fall of American humor."

VII

In addition to his talents as writer and artist, Thurber was one of the world's great talkers. "If he had never drawn a cartoon or written a word . . . he might still have made his mark as a great conversationalist in the class of Dr. Johnson or Bernard Shaw," observed *The Guardian* in its obituary essay.[8] Peter De Vries's account of Thurber's only public lecture gives a striking picture of the mastertalker in action. In his later years, Thurber did as much talking as writing, and he developed the interview-monologue into an art form, an oral performance which was part structured essay and part improvisation. In the interview with Plimpton and Steele, Thurber is his own critic, the artist as autobiographer, talking about his literary tastes, the craft of writing, his own work habits, the people who influenced him, and the state of humor in the modern world. W. J. Weatherby's 1961 interview is a vivid image of the older Thurber—gloomy, witty, indignant, embarked upon a stream of talk that seemed to be part of "an interior monologue that has been going on now for sixty-six years."

Summing up as versatile an artist as Thurber is not easy, but Paul Jennings, in "Man Against Monster," suggests some of the reasons for his importance as an interpreter of twentieth-century life; and E. B. White, in *The New Yorker*'s obituary tribute, beautifully evokes the qualities of mind and imagination which gave his work its special stamp:

> His mind was never at rest, and his pencil was connected to his mind by the best conductive tissue I have ever seen in action. The whole world knows what a funny man he was, but you had to sit next to him day after day to understand the extravagance of his clowning, the wildness and subtlety of his thinking, and the intensity of his interest in others and his sympathy for their dilemmas—dilemmas that he instantly enlarged, put in focus, and made immortal . . . .

The world Thurber created is both intensely American and enduringly universal. Although he wrote no single masterpiece like *Huckleberry Finn* or *Don Quixote,* his prose and his drawings, taken together, give us an image of life so original and so outrageously true that his place among the great comic writers seems already to be assured.

8 "Obituary—James Thurber," November 3, 1961, p. 5.

PART ONE

Traditions

From Columbus to New York

by John Seelye

Thurber was first, last and always a writer, though not at the start a very promising one, and his final emergence was not only long delayed, it was the result of very special circumstances. Without *The New Yorker,* there would have been no Thurber People, no Walter Mitty, and especially, no Thurber Dog. Yet, Thurber of *The New Yorker* was also Thurber of Columbus, Ohio, the town in which he was born in 1894, and in which he grew to young manhood. E. B. White understood him best; in his eulogy of his old friend and colleague he wrote:

> His waking dreams and his sleeping dreams commingled shamelessly and uproariously; Ohio was never far from his thought, and when he received a medal from his home state in 1953, he wrote, "The clocks that strike in my dreams are often the clocks of Columbus." It is a beautiful sentence and a revealing one.

Thurber remained a boy from Ohio, and to understand this is to understand a lot about Thurber and what he represents in American literature.

Like so many New York journalists, Thurber came out of the west, bringing with him a western sensibility. The founder of the backtrailing movement was William Dean Howells, who came to Boston from Ohio, ending up in New York at *Harper's.* Surely the most famous case is Harold Ross, the wild and woolly young editor from the far west who founded the magazine which quickly became the type and symbol of New York sophistication. It is not hard to explain why Manhattan has always held an attraction for bright young men from the west. Movies and novels have been written about it: from Ben Franklin to Thomas Wolfe, literature is full of examples proving that the city is a great catalyst of genius. When you realize Donald Barthelme—in many ways Thurber's successor at *The New Yorker*—is from east Texas, you have it in a nutshell.

Thurber also belongs to another great literary tradition, begun by Mark Twain and continued down through Barthelme. Though Thurber's satire would seem to resemble the eastern school of the mannerist absurd—the continuity of Stephen Leacock, Robert Benchley, and S. J. Perelman—there is a wild, Dionysian spirit hiding beneath the mask of Apollo, which like those clocks of Columbus is associated with Thurber's dreams of home. From his college days on, Thurber admired Henry James's mastery of style, but in his heart's core he was much closer to Mark Twain. Like both writers, Thurber was a wounded and a divided soul. In his case the wound was real as well as psychic: as a child, he was blinded in one eye by an arrow. Naturally rambunctious, he was forced into shyness by his handicap and was never able to play the games enjoyed by other Ohio boys, though he remained a lifelong sports fan. The double role was reinforced by his family life: Thurber grew up in a solid, middle-class Ohio household, yet the Thurbers were slightly out of kilter. The father was something of a dreamer and an ineffectual politician, while the mother was a decided extrovert, a nonstop talker with a flair for dramatics.

Strong mothers and weak fathers have produced a number of American comedians and presidents. Mark Twain also came from such a background, and though Thurber did not grow up into a tradition of southwestern humor, . . . western dime novels were his favorite childhood reading, and . . . his earliest attempts at writing were in that wild though stereotyped genre. Thurber also loved comic strips, particularly those which, like "The Toonerville Trolley," emphasized mayhem and chaos, or those, like Clare Briggs's "When a Feller Needs a Friend," which nostalgically portrayed kids growing up in rural America. [Charles] Holmes does not mention the influence of early silent movies, but these too must have had their impact. Certainly Thurber's best sketches based on his childhood experiences—the commingling of waking and sleeping dreams with memories of Columbus—are heavily derived from both comic strips and silent comedies of the Keystone sort. If the characteristically ineffectual Thurber man resembles James's middle-aged anti-heroes, so also does he derive from Clare Briggs's Casper Milquetoast. All of this is an equivalent of Mark Twain's sources in 19th-century popular culture.

Like Twain also, Thurber was a perpetual adolescent, whose immaturity manifested itself in many ways. Because of his inhibitions, he was a late bloomer, hanging back at each important stage in his life. While a freshman at Ohio State, he continued to write for his old high school magazine, and it was only the benevolent patronage of Elliott Nugent that got him involved in the social and literary life of the university. His college career was irregular, and rather than remain behind when his friends graduated, he left without a diploma, spending the war years as a code clerk in France. During this period he kept up contact with Nugent, writing embarrassingly naive and preposterously literary letters, quixotically Jamesian in their view of Europe. At the same time, he was sending letters home which, as Holmes points out, are in the vein of George not Irving Babbitt, full of by-gosh-and-by-gollies and reminiscent of the sports writing he had done in college. The clocks of Columbus seem to have been on his socks as well as in his dreams.

When he returned to Columbus after the war, Thurber took a job with the Dispatch, but he also wrote dramas and musical comedies for university players. They were derivative and unimaginative, like most of Thurber's early stuff. Though he hated the nuts-and-bolts aspect of newspaper reporting, his most promising work during these years was a column, "Credos and Curios," in which he began to develop a comic line in imitation of a local newspaper humorist. But his ambition was to become a dramatist or novelist. His marriage to Althea Adams, a woman of strong personality and cultural aspirations, led to a path, hardly primrose, out of Columbus to New York City and finally, in 1925, to France once again. This stay lasted less than a year, and was mostly spent working for the Paris *Herald Tribune*,* but it seems to have convinced Thurber that he was not another Henry James. When he returned to New York he took a job with the *Post*, leaving Althea for the time being in Europe.

Thurber had not yet found himself, and, strictly speaking, he never did. As Elliott Nugent had rescued him from anonymity at Ohio State, so E. B. White discovered him in New York. Having met him at a party, White took him to meet Harold Ross who, under the mistaken impression that the two men were old friends, hired Thurber on the spot, as managing editor, under yet another mistaken impression that Thurber had great organizational powers. Thurber soon disabused him of that notion and became a staff writer for the magazine. Under the stern eye of Ross and the gentler influence of White, he received the stylistic trimming and shaping

* Actually, the Paris edition of the Chicago *Tribune* [Ed.].

he had always needed and up to then had lacked. He developed the terse, balanced, ironic but essentially journalistic line which made him, White, and *The New Yorker* famous.

If *The New Yorker* atmosphere compressed Thurber's style, it also released something, and the strange alloy of aesthete and sportswriter suddenly began to demonstrate new and surprising strengths. The marriage with Althea continued, but not quite as before. Soon Thurber was using it as material for his stories about the long war between the sexes. He began to draw strange, improbable cartoons about seals and dogs, about mild men and wild women. And he began to dream those dreams about growing up absurdly in Ohio, giving vent to that long pent-up spirit of chaos and fantasy. The clocks of Columbus began to chime at last, and it was always 13 o'clock.

Thurber never completely exorcised his old demons, and even after a second, successful marriage to Helen Wismer, he continued his fits of drunken rage and his pathetic acts of contrition the morning after. Like Mark Twain, his warm heart could boil over with wrath, for he was both childish and a child, which is the secret of the weakness and the strength of both these men. Always a dreamer, his dreams were more often than not nightmares on the border of madness. In his old age, racked by disease and incapacitated by blindness, Thurber became a sort of resident western curmudgeon, snarling at a changing world he could not comprehend. But during the thirties and forties, his essentially western voice spoke through parables of exquisite texture, giving form to the spirit of wildness which redeems his early mistakes and his later failures. If Thurber heard the clocks of Columbus in his dreams, it was because he spent his days in New York City.

The Urbanization of Humor

by *Walter Blair*

In no other type of contemporary American writing are the changes in American society during the early years of the century more apparent than in our humor. Our chief humorists until the 1920's were all rustic or western. Since the 1920's, by contrast, our famous humorists have been urban.

Created by Benjamin Franklin early in the eighteenth century, Poor Richard Saunders led a procession of prodigiously popular humorous characters who, for two centuries, delighted nationwide audiences and often even shaped political decisions. Poor Richard had the essential traits of these characters. He was a countryman, and the best-loved humorous pundits showed by their dialect and their subject matter their farm or frontier origins. Poor Richard was uneducated but so acute and so experienced in the ways of the world that he could make witty comments which a nation worshiping what it called "horse sense" vastly appreciated. So it was with later vernacular humorists. There were Davy Crockett, coonskin frontier congressman, and Lowell's Yankee farmer Hosea Biglow, who his creator said personified "common-sense vivified and heated by conscience." There was H. W. Shaw's Ohio bumpkin, Josh Billings, whose creed was, "You have got to be wize [he spelled it with a z] before you can be witty." There was Mark Twain, creator of the Missouri ragamuffin Huck Finn and of the Connecticut Yankee, Hank Morgan—both, as Mark said, "ignoramuses" so far as book learning was concerned, but both so blessed with gumption that they could commune shrewdly.

The last giant in this procession of homespun humorists was Will Rogers, Oklahoma-born cowboy. "I've been eatin' pretty regular," said Will, "and the reason . . . is because I've stayed an old country boy." Thanks to varied media—syndicated newspaper columns, moving pictures, the radio—Will became more widely known than any of his predecessors in the tradition. But with his death in 1935 —a symbolically appropriate one in an airplane crash—the procession ended. Since then some old-time humorists have won some prominence. An exceptional Harry Golden, aided by the timeliness of many of his preachments, could score a remarkable success—three best-selling books of humorous commentaries in a row. Nevertheless, during the quarter century since Rogers' death, no humorist of his type with an iota of his prominence has arisen.

During his last years, Rogers was actually an anachronism who offered proof that old humorous traditions die hard. Widespread education had led many Americans to believe that book learning, which old-time humorists had scorned, was a better guide to wisdom than horse sense. The incongruity between ignorance and insight, our oldest joke, was no longer sure-fire. The rural and frontier civilizations which had nurtured dialect humorists were being replaced by an urban civilization lacking respect for men who talk in the vernacular. Already, humor of a new and very different sort was burgeoning.

The magazine which would be largely responsible for the rise of this new humor, even before its start in 1925, disavowed interest in rural and small-town readers so important as part of the humorists' audience in the past:

> THE NEW YORKER [said the Prospectus] will be the magazine which is not edited for the old lady in Dubuque. It will not be concerned in what she is thinking about. . . . THE NEW YORKER is a magazine avowedly published for a metropolitan audience and thereby will escape an influence which hampers most national publications. It expects a considerable national circulation, but this will come from persons who have a metropolitan interest.

Harold Ross, the author of the Prospectus, as editor, dominated the course of *The New Yorker*—the only important American humorous magazine since 1939—until his death in 1951. Not surprisingly, therefore, the announcement accurately forecast the magazine's history. And not surprisingly, *The New Yorker* attracted and sponsored four outstanding modern humorists, all with a distinctly urban flavor.

Clarence Shepard Day (1874–1935), Robert Benchley (1889–1945), James G. Thurber (1894–1961), and Sidney Joseph Perelman (1904–   ), all rose to prominence in the 1920's and are still appreciatively read. And though they did not entirely break with the past—no humorist does this—they did write humor based upon assumptions and emphasized techniques quite different from those of older humorists. They also employed new techniques.

Day, the son of a Wall Street broker, worked in the Stock Exchange after graduating from Yale, served in the U. S. Navy during the Spanish-American War, then became a journalist and a writer of sketches, essays, and books. Not, however, until he wrote a series of family reminiscences for *The New Yorker* and other magazines did he find his best and most popular vein. *God and My Father, Life with Father,* and *Life with Mother* (1932, 1935, 1937) were best sellers; a dramatization based upon them had a record run as a play and reincarnation as a successful motion picture.

Father, as Day pictured him, could have been an old-fashioned horse-sense philosopher if he had had a rural upbringing and had learned to say wise things in a witty way. Like Poor Richard, he has arrived at firm opinions about what is right on the basis of keen thinking and experience. He courageously takes stands and announces them. He is irked by those who carry on "all the chuckle-headed talk and rascality in business and politics":

> He was always getting indignant about them, and demanding that they be stamped out. . . . And twice a day, regularly, he would have a collision, or bout, with the newspaper; it was hard to see why God had made so many damned fools. . . . I would try to persuade him . . . to accept the world as it was and adapt himself to it, since he could scarcely expect to . . . change the whole earth single-handed. Father listened to this talk with suspicion. . . .

God Himself does not awe this rugged individualist: "he seemed to envisage a God in his own image. A God who had small use for emotionalism and who prized strength and dignity. . . . Father and God . . . usually saw eye to eye."

Father's resemblance to ancient rustic oracles is obvious. But his depicter's tone contrasts sharply with that of nineteenth-century authors picturing similar characters. The earlier authors—a Mark Twain picturing a Huck Finn, let us say—admired such characters and shared their attitudes. Day, though fond of Father, regards him as a quaint figure of a bygone era; he questions his standards, laughs at his judgments, satirizes his outmoded ways. In most stories, Father's "antagonists" are an irresponsible, flutter-brained family. They don't know what they're doing; they bumble and blunder. But Father fails to get what he wants; the family flounders to triumph. Mother in particular, conniving, not overly careful with truth, unsystematic, amoral, constantly outwits him. The contrast is particularly clear in one story in which an old Yankee trick is assigned to Mother as she fights a battle in the continuous war with Father about household accounts. The old-time Yankee cheated his victim because he was shrewd enough to devise the trick. Mother, on the contrary, manages to get away with the operation because she is illogical enough to stumble upon this way of outwitting her spouse. And Day leaves no doubt that he prefers Mother's way of doing things.

Benchley, Thurber and Perelman, all like Day, depict different characters but similarly rebel against ancient standards. The nineteenth-century humorous ancestors of this trio, significantly, were foils for the horse-sensible characters. They were the simpletons, the characters who took the wrong attitudes. Hosea Biglow's foil, for instance, was Birdofredum Sawin, a stupid rascal who was taken in by the wartime fanfare which Hosea scornfully attacked. Mark Twain had a good name for this group—"Inspired Idiots." Others called them "literary comedians." They were as invariably wrong about current problems as horse-sensible characters were right.

"The literary comedians," says Bernard De Voto, "presented themselves as Perfect Fools, whereas our [modern] comedians present themselves as Perfect Neurotics. There is no other difference." This may be true; but the difference is revolutionary.

Robert Benchley was an important contributor to *The New Yorker,* to other magazines and newspapers, to the profits of publishers of his collected pieces in fifteen books, and even to those of moving picture companies which filmed nearly fifty "shorts" in which he delivered monologues. In Benchley's very popular writings, and as a movie actor, he constantly assumed the role of a "Perfect Neurotic." The character he pretends to be is prevented from doing harmless things he'd like to do—leave a party when he wants, smoke a cigarette, wear a white suit, pick flowers, and so on. The frustrations have given this character phobias and complexes which he shows at work. A reader is not surprised to find this assumed character ticking off the symptoms of dementia praecox and finding that he has all of them.

"Some of this," writes Benchley's son, "was exaggerated, but not as much as might be supposed. Benchley was a highly subjective writer, and most of what he wrote was conditioned by his feelings about himself." This modern humorist, then, exaggerates—as did old-time humorists. But whereas the oldsters exaggerated the difficulties which they had to overcome and their ability to cope with them, Benchley exaggerates the smallness of his difficulties and his inability to cope with them. And the author's own troubles are like those of his comic character. J. Bryant III subtitles his profile of the humorist "A Study in Professional Frustration," and indicates that Benchley's conception of himself is of a man constantly humiliated and defeated by trifles: ". . . he sees himself . . . not [as] the master of high comedy, but the victim of low tragedy. King Lear loses a throne; Benchley loses a filling. Romeo breaks his heart; Benchley breaks his shoelace. They are annihilated: he is humiliated. And to his humiliations there is no end." Benchley's humor constantly makes use of such humiliations and the assumed character's failure to handle trifling problems. He speaks of working in "the dementia praecox field." Bryant notices that "Every page of his books is riddled with . . . pitfalls for sanity. Madness so dominates the landscape of his humor that a second reading is necessary to recognize its other features."

Milder, temporary, or even violent and permanent aberrations had been far from unusual in the older humor. Many literary comedians made people laugh at their "inspired idiocy." But the difference between the assumed character and the character of his creator was an important incongruity. James Russell Lowell played up the differences between himself—sane, logical, sound in his attitudes—and Birdofredum Sawin—mildly mad, illogical, unsound in his attitudes. The contrast made for irony, and the irony often made for satire. Just as Clemens stood apart from his wrong-headed Pap Finn while Pap lauded racial discrimination, and thereby attacked an attitude which Clemens abhorred, many literary comedians made the "I" in their writings obviously, comically, and satirically different from his creator.

The new emphasis was not on differences but on resemblances. Benchley exaggerates what he believes are his own qualities. And the expectation is that instead of feeling superior to the comic character, the reader will identify with that character, and sympathize with him. "The fellow," he'll say, "suffers from much the same frustrations, the same fears, the same incompetency I suffer from." He'll join the assumed character in being irritated by all the self-confident people he encounters: efficiency experts, go-getters, club women, scientists—all those well-adjusted (and quite probably self-deceived) clods. Clarence Day's Father is a character who definitely belongs to the enemy forces; Benchley would align himself with Mother.

James G. Thurber worked on several newspapers before beginning, in 1927, an association with *The New Yorker* that continued till his death. He published several popular books and invaded Broadway and the movies.

Thurber's discussion of the nature of humor shows immediately his kinship with Benchley:

> The things we laugh at are awful while they are going on, but get funny when we look back. And other people laugh because they've been through it too. . . . I think humor is the best that lies closest to the familiar, to that part of the familiar which is humiliating, distressing, even tragic. Humor is a kind of emotional chaos told about calmly and quietly in retrospect. There is always a laugh in the utterly familiar. . . . People can laugh out of a kind of mellowed self-pity as well as out of superiority.

The humiliation, the emotional chaos, are reminiscent of the misadventures of the "I" in Benchley's pieces. The identification of the reader with the suffering character is specific. Thurber adds that the events are "told about calmly and quietly in retrospect"— a shrewd comment which also applies to Benchley's way of telling about his emotional experiences.

A fine illustration is a portion of Thurber's story of what happened in Columbus, Ohio, the day the dam broke:

> The only possible means of escape for us was to flee the house, a step which grandfather sternly forbade, brandishing his old army sabre in his hand. "Let the sons———come!" he roared. Meanwhile hundreds of people were streaming by our house in wild panic, screaming, "Go east! Go east!" We had to stun grandfather with the ironing board. Impeded as we were by the inert form of the old gentleman—he was taller than six feet and weighed almost a hundred and seventy pounds—we were passed, in the first half mile, by practically everybody else in the city. Had grandfather not come to, at the corner of Parsons Avenue and Town Street, we would unquestionably have been overtaken and engulfed by the roaring waters—that is, if there had *been* any roaring waters.

Quel dommage! But what calm, what quietude the author manifests in writing about the events! There is no mention of the narrator's attitude: with Hemingwayesque restraint, he writes not about the emotion but the happenings which produce the emotion. An important disparity is that between the harrowing happenings and the objectivity which marks their description.

The fact that this is a passage in what playfully purports to be an autobiography, *My Life and Hard Times,* at least based upon personal experiences, suggests that Thurber, like Benchley, tends to identify himself in essential ways with his first-person narrator. And the author's description of "humorists" shows that they qualify to write Thurberian humor by living as their characters also live:

> They lead . . . an existence of jumpiness and apprehension. . . . [They] have a genius for getting into minor difficulties: they walk into the wrong apartments, they drink furniture polish for stomach bitters, they drive theirs cars into the prize tulip beds of haughty neighbors. . . .
>
> Such a writer moves restlessly wherever he goes, ready to get the hell out at the drop of a pie-pan or the lift of a skirt. His gestures are the ludicrous reflexes of the maladjusted; his repose is the momentary inertia of the nonplussed. . . . He talks largely about small matters and smally about great affairs.

This characterizes "the humorist"; it also characterizes the protagonists in Thurber's pieces and their adventures. In his guise of pictorial artist, Thurber portrays similar characters: his men "are frustrated, fugitive beings; at times they seem vaguely striving to get out of something without being seen (a room, a situation, a state of mind), at other times they are merely perplexed and too humble or meek to move." Like Benchley's character, they are baffled both by people and by inanimate objects.

Benchley testifies to S. J. Perelman's leadership in "the dementia praecox field." Perelman, another *New Yorker* star, has pictured his alter ego in a guise much like those of Benchley and Thurber: he too is frustrated and put upon; he too is helpless in a hostile world. Even more than they he is victimized by free association: "The color drained from my face, entered the auricle, shot up the escalator, and issued from the ladies' and misses' section into the housewares department," he reports.

His assumed character's distinctions are two: First, he tries to swagger, to brazen things out. A man of less than ordinary presence, he deceives himself into believing that he's a handsome dog. "I am a fairly typical Yankee," he modestly asserts, "who looks like Gary Cooper, sings like Frank Sinatra and dances like Fred Astaire . . ." He describes himself as "this man, who by sheer poise and magnetism had surmounted the handicap of almost ethereal beauty. . . ." A man of limited intelligence, he tries to impress one with his learning. He dots his pages with showy French, German and Italian phrases, with exotic names for clothing or strange dishes.

Second, the character he assumes has been brain-washed by mass media. He believes advertisements concocted by Madison Avenue

slickers. He accepts as actuality the fantastic world of current magazine fiction, the movies, even television. The delight and the horror
of his style is that it constantly takes off into the Never-Never Land
of the mass media. After reading an advertisement, he follows with
complete trust its suggestions. After reading a story or seeing a
motion picture he concocts fantasies even more absurd than those
which have unfolded before him. Often these are cliché-bedecked
phrases or sentences: "Diamonds of the finest water gleamed at the
throats of women whose beauty put the gems to shame," he claims,
"and if each was not escorted by a veritable Adonis, he was at least
a Greek." Again, "Not a muscle flickered in my lean jaw . . . as
our little procession moved past the group of cattlemen lounging
outside the Golden Girl Saloon, and their pithy comments had long
since died away before I permitted myself a muttered 'Swine.' "

As in reading Benchley and Thurber, the reader sees in the assumed character here a man much like himself. In some ways,
Perelman's vision of what we tend to be is the most frightening of
all. His is a comic version of Huxley's *Brave New World,* or Orwell's *1984.*

He is not the only writer in this group whose comic representatives are allied with more serious fictions. Peter DeVries years ago
pointed out an extraordinary resemblance between Thurber's little man and that creation of T. S. Eliot, J. Alfred Prufrock—"The
same dominating sense of Predicament . . . the same immersion in
weary minutiae, the same self-disparagement, the same wariness
. . . the same fear, in summary, that someone . . . will 'drop a
question on his plate.' " The comparison might be extended to
include many characters in the modern fiction, the figure Sean
O'Faolain sees as "the anti-Hero":

> He is always represented as groping, puzzled, cross, mocking, frus-
> trated, isolated in his manful or blundering attempts to establish
> his own personal, suprasocial codes. . . . Whether he is weak,
> brave, brainy or bewildered he is always out on his own. Which
> is why, in those fateful twenties, writers quite deliberately began
> . . . to dig out private caves, or air-raid shelters, of their own,
> and there started to compose private satires, laments, fantasies and
> myths in the effort to fill the vacuum left by the death of the social
> Hero with asocial rebels, martyrs, misfits, minor prophets, or, in
> short, with aberrants and anti-Heroes.

The relationship between Thurber's humor and this serious view
of humanity becomes clear when one considers Thurber's personal
nonhumorous statement about his own view of man:

For some curious reason Man has always assumed that he is the highest form of life in the universe. There is, of course, nothing with which to sustain this view. Man is simply the highest form of life on his own planet. His superiority rests on a thin and chancy basis: he has the trick of articulate speech and out of this, slowly and laboriously, he has developed the capacity of abstract reasoning. Abstract reasoning, in itself, has not benefited Man so much as instinct has benefited the lower animals. . . . In giving up instinct and going in for reasoning, Man has aspired higher than the attainment of natural goals; he has developed ideas and notions; he has monkeyed around with concepts. The life to which he was naturally adapted he has put behind him; in moving into the alien and complicated sphere of Thought and Imagination he has become the least well-adjusted of all the creatures of the earth, and hence the most bewildered. . . . Man . . . is surely farther away from the Answer than any other animal this side of the ladybug.

The humor of Thurber and his contemporaries is, I suggest, a comic representation of man in this grim situation. Grim, yes, if humor is taken literally, as this playful self-criticism never should be. Nurtured by a free press, native American humor has always been a purge for worries and tribulations—the struggles of a democratic nation to get going, frontier hardships, wartime tragedies, the upheavals accompanying the shift from an agrarian, rural society to an industrial, urban society. In that sense, Day, Benchley, Thurber and Perelman write in an old and honorable tradition. Also, their assumptions and beliefs are in tune with attitudes of their era. But the different nature of their assumptions and the great change in their beliefs have led them to write humor strikingly different indeed from that of the past.

James Thurber's Little Man
and Liberal Citizen

by Norris Yates

The Humor of Despair

In his nonfictional essays Thurber sometimes wears the mask of the same figure who cowers in his fiction, with the minor difference that the Little Man of the essays often writes for a living. As a writer, he may easily be portrayed as a wise fool and sad clown:

> Authors of such pieces ["light" pieces running from a thousand to two thousand words] have, nobody knows why, a genius for getting into minor difficulties: they walk into the wrong apartments, they drink furniture polish for stomach bitters, they drive their cars into the prize tulip beds of haughty neighbors, they playfully slap gangsters, mistaking them for old school friends. To call such persons "humorists," a loose-fitting and ugly word, is to miss the nature of their dilemma and the dilemma of their nature. The little wheels of their invention are set in motion by the damp hand of melancholy.

Saddened by his own ineptitude and by his encounters with women, psychiatrists, business, bureaucracy, gadgets, and automobiles,[1] this *persona* was further depressed by the disasters of the nineteen-thirties at home and abroad. "I suspect that nothing is going to get us

"James Thurber's Little Man and Liberal Citizen." From Norris Yates, *The American Humorist: Conscience of the Twentieth Century* (Ames, Iowa: the Iowa State University Press, 1964). Copyright © 1964 by the Iowa State University Press, Ames, Iowa. Reprinted by permission of the author and the publisher. The selection reprinted here is only a portion of Professor Yates's chapter.

[1] In case anyone should confuse Thurber with his *persona* of Little Man, a comment by Wolcott Gibbs is worth quoting: "The essence of Thurber is such that in any real contest of personalities everyone else would be well advised to take to the hills." Qu. in "Thurber and his Humor," *Newsweek*, XLIX (February 4, 1957), 56.

anywhere," Thurber wrote in 1937, in opposition to those who felt optimistic about the international situation.[2] Elsewhere his comments place him in the broad streams of literary naturalism and pessimism. Man, he says, is merely a part of nature and not necessarily the best part at that:

> Man is simply the highest form of life on his own planet. His superiority rests on a thin and chancy basis: he has the trick of articulate speech and out of this, slowly and laboriously, he has developed the capacity of abstract reasoning. . . . Man has aspired higher than the attainment of natural goals; he has developed ideas and notions; he has monkeyed around with concepts. The life to which he was naturally adapted he has put behind him; in moving into the alien and complicated sphere of Thought and Imagination he has become the least well-adjusted of all the creatures of the earth, and hence the most bewildered . . .

Clarence Day had said something like that in *This Simian World* but had not altogether rejected reason and hope. Thurber's attitude has some of the blackness of Don Marquis, and shows affinity also with writers outside the sphere of humor who disparage reason and stress the maladjustment of man when he moves beyond his animal origins. Sherwood Anderson envied the lot of children and illiterate Negroes; the crew in O'Neill's *The Hairy Ape* advise Yank to "Drink, don't think!" Hemingway's Nick Adams and Frederick Henry are better off when they are fishing, swimming, drinking, or fornicating than when the wheels of their reflection are spinning. Being more cerebral than Yank and more inhibited than Hemingway's males, Thurber's characters find little solace in drink—though not from lack of trying—and their sexual ventures seldom get beyond wishful thinking. But they too are specimens of nature; the introductory quotation for *The Beast in Me* concerns "the beast inside, the beast that haunts the moonlit marges of the mind."

Charles Child Walcutt has emphasized the intimate relationship between naturalism and Freudianism,[3] and an orthodox Freudian would see Thurber's Little Man as tormented by the conflict between the unconscious "beast" of sex and the repression of it by the superego, which is shaped and dominated by this man's "civilized" environment. The repressed animal finds its outlet in anxieties, fixations, and obsessions. Basically, society is at fault for repressing rather than channeling the primary urge.

[2] James Thurber, "Pepper for the Belgians," *New Yorker*, XIII (December 18, 1937), 20.
[3] Walcutt, *American Literary Naturalism*, pp. 20–21.

As hinted earlier, some of Thurber's ideas about sex and personality are not necessarily in conflict with those of Freud. Thurber feels that the male animal is unduly repressed by his environment, an environment which includes another animal, his wife, who both abets and conceals her ruthlessness by means of more resolution, solicitude for her mate, and competence in the small matters of everyday living than he shows. Part of his environment is also a society going mad through a misapplication of technology; so-called neurosis is often merely "a natural caution in a world made up of gadgets that whir and whine and whiz and shriek and sometimes explode." Thurber differs from Freud in ignoring the Oedipus complex, whereas Freud regarded this as the major component of sex. He also differs in feeling that it is futile for man to expect to throw off his repressions or even to sublimate them satisfactorily. The civilized (or repressing and repressed) elements in the Little Man's character and environment often have the same cosmic finality as the natural traits. Thurber's people rarely succeed in changing any aspect of either their surroundings or themselves, and such "adjustment" as the male achieves usually comes only through complete withdrawal, as in the cases of Mitty, and of Grandfather in *My Life and Hard Times.* . . .

Several of the fables carry a message also found in *Is Sex Necessary?* and *Let Your Mind Alone*: namely, the naturalistic theme that man, in trying to act as if he were above his place in nature's order, has muddled himself into disaster. A "seal" leaves his natural habitat to join a circus; when he returns home to impress the stay-at-homes he tries to swim, but

> . . . he was so hampered by his smart city clothes, including a pair of seventeen-dollar shoes, that he began to founder at once. Since he hadn't been in swimming for three years, he had forgot what to do with his flippers and tail, and he went down for the third time before the other seals could reach him. They gave him a simple but dignified funeral.
>
> *Moral:* Whom God has equipped with flippers should not monkey around with zippers.

Likewise, a crow falls in love with an oriole and "pleaded his cause —or should we say cawed his pleas?" All he gets by this is the loss of his proper crow-wife. "Moral: Even the llama should stick to mamma." A tiger and a leopard stage a prize fight and end up killing each other. "Moral: If you live as humans do, it will be the end of you." But since the animal kingdom can match the human race in showing an irrational urge to destroy itself—witness the lemmings—there is little consolation or wisdom to be found in the nonhuman world, except for the courage and tranquillity of certain dogs.

Although Thurber meant *The Last Flower* (1939) to be a message of hope, it is easier to find the central idea of this sequence of cartoons and captions, done hastily on the eve of World War II, in the depiction of civilization as doomed to emerge from one meaningless cycle of self-destruction only to plunge into another. This fable might be termed one of those "Ironic points of light" which W. H. Auden in "September 1, 1939" said were flashing out "wherever the Just/Exchange their messages." [4] Any optimistic implication is overshadowed by the somber content of Thurber's sequence and by its implicit determinism.

One of The Just

A pessimistic naturalism has thus permeated Thurber's depiction of the Little Man, but in the late nineteen-thirties, as the economic depression persisted and war began to threaten, he began to say things about public affairs that call for classifying his literary double also with the heirs of the Progressive "New Citizen," that is, with the liberals of the thirties and forties and with the active opponents of McCarthyism in the frightened fifties. In the anger of *The Last Flower* itself one senses—again, in Auden's words—"an affirming flame" of zeal and hope which is scarcely consistent with despair, and for over a quarter of a century Thurber was outspoken in his attacks on authoritarianism of both left and right.

In the "Preface" to *My Life and Hard Times*, Thurber had insisted that as a writer he was just another Little Man with little interests. . . .

This preface written in 1933 was outdated by 1940 as a reliable source of information about Thurber's interests. In the latter year, he wrote a column for *PM*, a militantly antifascist daily in New York City, "twice a week until I went into a nervous tail spin following my fifth eye operation." [5] The play *The Male Animal*, by

---

[4] From "September 1, 1939," by W. H. Auden. Copyright 1940 by W. H. Auden. Reprinted from *The Collected Poetry of W. H. Auden*, by permission of Random House, Inc.

[5] Thurber, *The Years with Ross*, p. 121.

Thurber and Elliott Nugent, was produced in the same year, and the playwrights proved that they most certainly did hear "the rumblings of the dynasties," especially those reverberations that sounded near home. This play has two rather awkwardly interwoven plots: in one of them Professor Tommy Turner is the usual confused Thurber husband, but in the other his integrity as a teacher makes him stick to his plan of reading in class the letter of Vanzetti about the significance of his own and his partner Sacco's execution, despite the threats of a Babbitt type of trustee that Tommy will be fired for this action. In standing up for academic freedom, Tommy is not merely a male animal but the liberal citizen behaving as a citizen ought to behave when freedom is threatened.

Some of the *Fables for Our Time* also suggest a citizen-writer for whom all is not lost, practicing the eternal vigilance cited by the forefathers as the price of liberty. In "The Birds and the Foxes," the latter animals "civilize" the geese and ducks, and "liberate" the orioles by killing and eating them. "Moral: Government of the orioles, by the foxes, and for the foxes, must perish from the earth." Even closer to the lesson of *The Male Animal* is the fable in which a gander is unjustly set upon because somebody has complimented him for being a "proper gander." Somebody else, however, thinks that this bird is being accused of propaganda. The ironic moral is: "Anybody who you or your wife thinks is going to overthrow the government by violence must be driven out of the country."

In certain nonhumorous pieces, Thurber also has shown his social and political involvement. He criticized *The Moon Is Down* (1942), John Steinbeck's novel about the Nazi conquest of Norway, for its allegedly sympathetic portrayal of the conquerors. Thurber declared in the *New Republic* (Clarence Day's old employers) that ". . . this book needs more guts and less moon," and that it softened the true story of "hell, horror and hopelessness." Neither here nor in his defense when criticized in his turn was there any of the naturalistic defeatism and passivity associated with the Little Man.[6] Naturalism was likewise in eclipse during a lecture on humor given in his native Columbus in 1953, where he said, "There used

---

[6] See "What Price Conquest?" *New Republic*, CVI (March 16, 1942), 370; "Correspondence" (March 30, 1942), 43. The controversy stirred up by Thurber's review is discussed by Peter Lisca, *The Wide World of John Steinbeck*, Rutgers University Press (New Brunswick, New Jersey, 1958), pp. 186–188, 305–306. Replying to one reader who called his review "a slap in the face," Thurber wrote, "I am sorry about that slap in the face. I didn't realize my hand was open."

to be men among us who could brandish the shield of humor with telling effect in the now sensitive area of politics and government . . . the H. L. Mencken of an earlier and bolder day, and the late Will Rogers, and William Allen White, and old Ed Howe . . ." Besides praising the militancy of two conservatives (Mencken and Howe), a New Dealer (Rogers), and a writer best classified as both and neither (White), Thurber threw a punch at McCarthyism with ". . . [comedy] sickens in the weather of intimidation and suppression, and such a sickness could infect a whole nation. The only rules comedy can tolerate are those of taste, and the only limitations those of libel." [7] In an interview given during the previous year, Thurber called himself "an Eisenhower man," [8] and his attitudes on McCarthyism and on the presidential election added up to those of a man who felt close to the middle of the political road but very much in that road—not off to one side, detached, paring his fingernails.

Thurber's humor in his last decade shows the same inconsistent mixture of despair and of militancy with its concomitant of hope. In *Further Fables for Our Time* (1956), one finds some of the older, skeptical pessimism about the human race—see "The Human Being and the Dinosaur"—but one also finds that at least ten out of the forty-seven fables in this book are disguised tracts in defense of free expression. In "The Peacelike Mongoose," an animal of that species is persecuted for his use of "reason and intelligence" by those who cry "Reason is six-sevenths of treason." Two more fables are likewise thrusts at McCarthyism: "The Trial of the Old Watchdog" and "Ivory, Apes, and People," but at least two of these *Further Fables* are satires of Soviet communism, which Thurber hated as much as he disliked professional Americanism ("The nature of humor is anti-communistic," he declared in his Ohio lecture). In *Lanterns and Lances* (1960), the pessimistic theme that man embodies the worst aspects of nature is prominent, but Thurber praises the late Elmer Davis, of whose New Deal and Fair Deal sympathies there was no doubt, and Edward P. Morgan, sponsored by the CIO-AF of L, for "intelligence, devotion to American ideals, courage, and

7 Thurber, *Thurber on Humor*, The Martha Kinney Cooper Ohioana Library Association (Columbus, Ohio, 1953), pp. 10–11; *Lanterns and Lances*, pp. 211–212. Cf. James Thurber, "The Case for Comedy," *Atlantic*, CCVI (November, 1960), 97–99.

8 Harvey Breit, "Talk with James Thurber," *New York Times Book Review*, June 29, 1952, p. 19, repr. in Breit, *The Writer Observed*, Collier Books (New York, 1961), p. 167.

wit." In this, his last book before his death, Thurber evidently felt these phenomena were still worth a few broken lances.

The liberal citizen would lead no forlorn hope either. In his "Foreword," the author says the perceptive will detect in these pieces "a basic and indestructible thread of hope. . . . It is lighter than you think."

Thurber's liberalism resembles that of Day and Benchley in being sharply limited by his middle-class angle of vision. Most of his neurotic males and females are suburbanites with hired "help" and summer cottages; people who earn their living with their hands are among the threats to this white-collar cocktail crowd. Mr. Monroe shrinks before the furniture movers; Walter Mitty is buffaloed by the parking-lot attendant; Mr. Pendly by garage mechanics, and several of Thurber's protagonists by waiters, maids, or butlers. In 1934 Thurber served on a committee for the welfare of waiters during a strike by these workers, but he admitted that he didn't have the slightest idea of what waiters do when they go home. In his essays, Thurber or rather his *persona*, has difficulty with waiters, office help, street-gang laborers, house-servants, and hired yardmen. Oftener than any humorist of note since Bangs, Thurber makes comedy out of "difficult" servants. The maid in *The Male Animal* is a nineteenth-century stereotype. If their employers are neurotic, Emma Inch, Barney Haller, and several Negro maids are "odd," cross-grained, stupid, or downright psychotic. The servants of the Thurber family in *My Life and Hard Times* usually seem even more unbalanced than their employers, and in a revealing piece called "A Friend of the Earth," Thurber's *alter ego* psychologically grapples with Zeph Leggins, a village roustabout, philosopher, and joker who can also be taken as a symbol of the author's rejection of crackerbarrel humor.

Only occasionally are the manual workers shown as mentally healthy, in contrast to the neurotic persons with more money and book-learning. One such worker is the cabdriver who tells Kirk in "One Is a Wanderer" that "I got a home over in Brooklyn and a wife and a couple kids, and, boy, I'm tellin' you that's the best place . . ." The point is not that Thurber makes a principle of relating neurosis to social class, but that nearly all manual workers in his writings are seen only from the viewpoint of their employers, and the author does not seem interested in any other viewpoint. When not butts of satire, they are mere foils for his educated, middle-class neurotics.

Two Types of Thurber Male

Thus, one of Thurber's masks has been that of a Little Man help-less in the grip of nature, his wife, and his own nature; the other, used somewhat less often, has been that of a militant of the Progres-sive–New Deal stamp. (One recalls that many Progressive–New Deal-ers were conservative in their values and liberal in their advocation of reforms to conserve those values.) The two attitudes existed simultaneously throughout Thurber's career, although most of his pessimistic pieces appeared in the earlier part of his career and most of his more optimistic pieces were written since about 1939. In 1953 he implied that even his satirical portraits of women had been made with a reformer's intent:

> Almost any century now Woman may lose her patience with black politics and red war and let fly. I wish I could be on earth then to witness the saving of our self-destructive species by its greatest crea-tive force. If I have sometimes seemed to make fun of Woman, I assure you it has only been for the purpose of egging her on.[9]

These statements may be mellow afterthoughts during a happy second marriage, but a contradiction remains between the view of man as a helpless bit of animated earth and the view that he can and ought to achieve his freedom and improve his lot. This con-tradiction is reduced but not resolved by the fact that Thurber's pessimistic determinism appears chiefly in his writings about per-sonal and domestic matters, whereas his belief in free will and free-dom crops out mainly in his pieces dealing with social and political topics. Rarely, as in *The Male Animal,* does he try to fuse the two realms of subject matter and the two philosophies, and when he does try, the result is not convincing either as ideology or as art.

In the work of Benchley one sees a family man and citizen who is seldom victorious and often defeated but who rarely gives up his theoretical hold on certain hard and fast values. In Thurber's writ-ing, this figure is more often driven over the brink to psychosis and separated from any sense of values. The *persona* who fights the liberal fight for a freedom he refuses to consider dead in theory or in practice is separate and distinct from the beaten-down Little Man. Faced with the dilemma of naturalism—the belief that man is an animal whose character and fate are predetermined by his heredity and his environment—and the contradictory need for some

---

[9] *Thurber on Humor,* p. 10; *Lanterns and Lances,* p. 211.

form of belief in free will and morality if one is to live harmoniously among one's fellows or to write humor, Thurber solved the problem no better than did Mencken. Mencken blithely ignored the dilemma; Thurber divided his conception of man and embodied each conception in a separate image inconsistent with the other. Ring Lardner too had suffered from the same ideological schizophrenia, but Lardner never warmed to the humanitarian tradition, and a nearly complete pessimism took hold of him. Don Marquis was affected by the same split, though his nagging wish that things might be better in spite of the naturalistic cosmos was born of religious idealism rather than secular humanitarianism. Marquis too attempted to disguise the problem by the use of more than one comic mask.

All these writers may be called pre-atomic pessimists, but since 1945, the dilemma with which they struggled has not changed in kind—only in urgency.[10]

10 A posthumous collection of Thurber's sketches, stories, and tributes to contemporaries is *Credos and Curios,* Harper and Row (New York, 1962). A comprehensive selection of his writings and drawings is Helen Thurber (comp.) *Vintage Thurber,* 2 vols., Hamish Hamilton (London, 1963). Thurber's writings have also furnished the material for two musical revues, *The Thurber Carnival* and *The Beast in Me.*

James Thurber: The Comic Prufrock

by Peter De Vries

It was on an evening in the late spring of 1938, at a banquet at the University of Chicago, while crawling around on my hands and knees under the speakers' table looking for Ford Madox Ford's glasses, that I first knew I was going to write an article on Thurber. It was a moment of murk and strain: I remember the women just standing there, and getting in my hair, most of which hung over one eye. I suppose there have been occasions when I looked even more like a Thurber drawing; but there has been none when I felt more like one. I have had this queer feeling of looking like a Thurber drawing on four distinct occasions in my life, counting the evening I failed to find Ford Madox Ford's glasses—or "glosses" as he said when he promptly singled me out from among the group of intellectuals as probably the ideal man to whom to report the loss of spectacles. The other times were: once when turning around to glare at a woman talking behind me at a concert; once while crawling around on the floor of a cold garage looking for a cotter pin while the neighbor lady whose car I was presumably going to fix, when I found it, hung around; and once reciting "No, no, go not to Lethe, neither twist wolf's bane" in a drug store to a girl who I found had turned to the menu.

I am not sure what poetic sensitivity is, but I am practically certain Thurber has got it. Though artists work in different forms there is a contemporary tissue which connects them, and the things they have in common spiritually are greater than the differences among them technically. Thurber has more in common with modern poets than, for instance, he has with any other present-day humorist you might mention.

I do not know whether the critical landlords of Axel's Castle—

our customary symbol for Symbolism—list him among the occupants
or not, or whether they are aware he is on the premises. It is that
house (to call a partial roll) through whose silences can be heard
the interminable scratching of the pen of Proust, and the sad sound
of his cough. Here Prufrock, lost in the fumes of introspection, lay
damned in the late afternoon. From its window Yeats saw the centaur stamp in the black wood, and Joyce labored mightily in its tow-
ers. If fancy and the imagination and "subjective" as opposed to
"objective" reality is the emphasis we are talking about, then Thurber can certainly be included. The filaments of individual sensibility
are seldom more sharply wrought, or more constantly manifest, than
in his work. The psychological nuance is rarely more intricately
drawn, even in those tidy sketches in which he is reducing it to absurdity. His inner states and private convolutions are, if not as profound, as skillfully projected as any. He may be least of the family—
indeed perhaps just a quizzical lodger cutting up in some remote
corner of the premises—but this is the address all right.

It is hard to think of anyone who more closely resembles the Prufrock of Eliot than the middle-aged man on the flying trapeze. This
preoccupied figure is Prufrock's comic counterpart, not in intensity
of course, but in detail. There is, for instance, the same dominating
sense of Predicament. The same painful and fastidious self-inven-
tory, the same detailed anxiety; the same immersion in weary minutiae, the same self-disparagement, the same wariness of the evening's
company. And the same fear, in summary, that someone—in Thurber's case a brash halfback or maybe even a woman—will "drop a
question on his plate." Prufrock, taking stock of himself, concludes
that he is no Prince Hamlet, "nor was meant to be"; is merely one
who will do

> To swell a progress, start a scene or two.
>
> .   .   .   .
>
> At times, indeed, almost ridiculous—
> Almost, at times, the Fool.

Thurber tells us that he is no Lord Jim, nor any character whatever
out of Conrad. Among the southern seas none guessed his minor
doom, though he sat in tropical cafes twitching his jaw muscles, in
the attempt to look inscrutable. Prufrock in his lush fantasies "heard
the mermaids singing, each to each." And concludes, "I do not think
that they will sing to me." Among the seductive islands Thurber
found no Tondelaya, or any facsimile thereof, offering to go to
pieces with him. Of the women he is terse:

They tried to sell me baskets.

If Eliot symbolizes his spiritual intricacies in terms of mythologi-
cal beings, so that we get the Eumenides lurking, at last, behind a
curtain in an English drawing room, Thurber can personify his own
modest nemeses in figures as concrete, always afraid he is "being
softly followed by little men padding along in single file, about a
foot and a half high, large-eyed and whiskered." This ability to pro-
ject the fanciful enables him to get pretty much the effect of poetry
itself. The banquet I mentioned stands out in my memory for one
other thing. It is a phrase in Carl Sandburg's talk: "Those who write
the poetry of an age, whether in verse or prose . . ." Enough. If
poetry is an essence produced by the discharge of the contents of the
Leyden jar of the nervous system (and it most certainly is not but at
this point we want one of those definitions which serve chiefly to
prove that poetry can't be defined) then Thurber has produced poetry in at least a few cases. Poetry is where you find it, and I find it in
The Black Magic of Barney Haller, one of the best of those exquisite
little sketches which see more drafts than many poems. You will remember it as the account of the caretaker whom storms follow home,
whom Thurber suspects of trafficking with the devil and exorcises
by incantations of Frost and Lewis Carroll.

The title of Eliot's poem is ironic—it is a "love song." It is certain
that Prufrock never got around to asking his lady the question: the
masculinity of this parched sophisticate seems specifically inopera-
tive. In that other landmark of Eliot's early period, *The Portrait
of a Lady,* the female is roundly satirized, but the narrator is singu-
larly unable to cope with her; there is a "sensation of being ill at
ease." Is there a sensation of which Thurber has given more repeated
illustration? The oppressed narrator of Eliot's poem has the feeling,
after climbing the stairs, of having "mounted on my hands and
knees." One can imagine what Thurber would have done with *that,*
had he included it in his series in which he illustrated famous poems.
It will be observed that in all of the instances in which I felt like a
Thurber drawing there were women around—behind me, in front
of me, and, most of all, above me. What contemporary disquiet has
he caught here? The woman satirized in *The Portrait of a Lady* was
trite, but she was alive and certainly operating conversationally, and
the women lampooned in Thurber are alive and operating too, at
their worst when they are a little too much like the preoccupied
men (like the woman who came up and announced to the man
shrinking in the chair: "I have a neurosis"), at their best possessing

a certain virility lacking in the male. They perch confidently on the arms of sofas, drag their men to bridge parties, drive cars well, are in the embalming game. The male is on the wane, corroded with introspection, deflated by all his own inefficient efficiency, without "strength to force the moment to its crisis," his love lyric in desuetude. There is a sketch in which Thurber does not want to go some place—out some place, perhaps a bridge party or something like that—and he says he would rather stay home. "That's the place for a man to be anyhow—home." It is not a long step from there to: "A man's place is in the home," a generalization the feminists of the hour might like to adopt as a battle cry.

Anybody who would rather not throw a javelin because Babe Didrikson could probably throw it farther, which is one of Thurber's reasons, is in a bad way. In *The Case Against Women* Thurber lists the reasons why he hates them, not, of course, that we don't, by this time, know. The boneless batter of the famous drawings is of course a caricature; but a caricature of a sharp contemporary sensation. Maybe it is only the first bug-eyed bewilderment of man startled and dazed by the little helpmate's first brisk emergence into the wide world. It is to be hoped that such is the case and that the notorious Thurber male, subsiding, in bed and chair and at last on the rug, in various postures of anthropoid humiliation, is not a preview of the shape of things to come.

There is another possible construction on the matter, intimated by Thurber himself, which, though not rich in consolation, is a little more palatable to the male. Thurber qualifies the often echoed forecast that we are going to pot, with the specification that man will go first. The cities in which he has so long conducted his business, contrived his morals and debauched his politics, and in which he has now grown futilely introspective, are to be taken over by the praying mantis and the steppe cat. But before that there will be an interlude in which the women will be in there pitching. That dwindling masculine first person singular who has not written a single amorous poem nearly as good as the famous "lovesong" in which Prufrock never got anywhere, will be in circumstances over which it were perhaps better not to speculate in too great detail. But woman's emergence, now dramatic, can be expected to go on apace. She is already everywhere in industry; she is in Congress, on the pulpit and, as has been noted, in the embalming game—standing ready to commit us to the earth. Women live longer, too. Studying the newspaper accounts of forty-three people who got to be more than a hundred, Thurber notes that thirty-seven are women and six men, and four of them were written about because they died. And the women were reported as having celebrated the day by chinning themselves, riding in airplanes and performing other feats too depressing to mention. The female's retention of vigor, straight-forwardness and the positive values is, perhaps, quite logical; for is she not more directly and intimately the custodian of life? It is Molly Bloom who closes the incredibly elaborate *Ulysses,* pulling the whole business back down to earth.

"The poet of *The Waste Land,*" writes Edmund Wilson, "is living half the time in the real world of contemporary London and half the time in the haunted wilderness of medieval legend." Thurber too is half the time God knows where. "One's head may be stored with literature but the heroic prelude of the Elizabethans has ironic echoes in modern London streets and modern London drawing rooms." Reality in Thurber undergoes filterings and transmutations as curious and as abrupt. He deflates famous poems with cruelly literal illustrations, achieving bathos as jolting as Eliot's:

> When lovely woman stoops to folly and
> Paces about her room again, alone,
> She smoothes her hair with automatic hand,
> And puts a record on the gramophone.

Confronted by details, moments, of that dull environment with which he is long weary of coping, he contrives his own little substitutions, and his transformer is always at work altering, to suit his fancy, the currents of experience. With characteristic self-deploration he admits to the inanity of many of the oddments that "slip by the guardian at the portal of his thoughts," but vouches for their tenacity. Thus

> A message for Captain Bligh
> And a greeting to Franchot Tone!

sung to a certain part of *For He's a Jolly Good Fellow,* occupied him for some time. A connoisseur of mispronunciation, he was happy when a malapropping domestic called the icebox "doom shaped," thus investing it with a quality which fascinated him for days, and by a similar alchemy exercised by Barney Haller, the caretaker already mentioned, there are warbs in the garrick, grotches in the wood and fletchers on the lawn—all details possessing a charm with which their real-life counterparts cannot compete. To make the transformation complete, the maid has only to step on his glasses. Then do the flags of South American republics fly over the roofs of Manhattan banks, cats cross the street in striped barrels, old women

with parasols walk through the sides of trucks, bridges rise "lazily
into the air like balloons." "The kingdom of the partly blind," he
assures us, jesting of his affliction, "is a little like Oz, a little like
Wonderland, a little like Poictesme." He never drives alone at night
"out of fear that I might turn up at the portals of some mystical
monastery and never return." He has but to do that, and the parallel
with Eliot is complete.

Now all these qualities in Thurber serve to illustrate again this
fact: that attitudes, details, elements, are intimated in poetry before
they are widely apparent in the general contemporary consciousness,
or in popular literature. The truly original poet is often prescient.
Swinging the classics, as our jazz bands now do, the fluid technique
of shuttling arbitrarily between the past and the present without
transition, of which novelists and playwrights now freely avail themselves, our pleasure in mimicry, all these and so many less tangible
elements in the climate of our time were contained and fore-
shadowed in a single poem which was called senseless when it first
came out. Poetry is sometimes an antenna by which the race detects
actualities at which it has not quite arrived.

The contempt of the man with both feet on the ground for the
artist with one of them in fantasy is familiar. Such a condition is
regarded as a schizoid separation from reality. The answer is of
course, simply, what do you mean by reality; and the point is an important one. I referred, with rather loose whimsicality I suppose, to
Thurber as jester in Axel's Castle, and his work may be a rivulet
running "individual sensibility" off into a kind of *reductio ad ab-
surdum*—not that some of the serious exponents of Symbolism
haven't already done so. But whatever the excesses of Symbolism
may have been, it has not only made a notable contribution to modern literature but by its emphasis on subjective experience has
helped us to a richer idea of what "reality" is. Just as poetry and
profit are where you find them, reality is what you make it. The angle of refraction according to the perceiving psyche is *always* there,
and the individual's extracting from the world around him consti-
tutes an experience that is itself a reality; a point which modern
artists have been trying to make for over a generation. It is to be admitted that Symbolism, falling prey to another of our many false
dualisms in its reaction to Naturalism, has sometimes gone to excesses, but we may hope, as Edmund Wilson suggests, that something of a healthier balance will be derived from a synthesis of the
two.

To get back a moment, before closing, to Thurber, whom we have left peering into the abyss, on all fours no doubt: We do not know that art and life will continue in the direction which he, in his peculiar way, has brought to such sharp emphasis. We do not know how events and literature, in their endless and intricate interaction, will condition the man of tomorrow, whether to more evaporating introversions or to new expansions. We know that the large pendulum which enables us to tick our little ticks keeps swinging. Prophecy is an easy and a dangerous thing, for thou knowest not which shall prosper, whether this or that, or whether they both shall be alike good. And as to women, if the Curtain is one day coming down, well, Thurber's own prediction that they will outlast men only bears out once more the fact that men, more sensitive organisms, are pioneers in everything, even decline. And we need not vex ourselves with the illusion that the sexes were ever anything but opposed (the literature Thurber might illustrate going back to Genesis—"The woman whom thou gavest to be with me, she gave me of the tree, and I did eat"), nor face our future oppressed by the extraneous consideration that it will be survived by gnats.

James Thurber and Henry James

by Edward Stone

That the late humorist Thurber (James) knew his way through darkest James (Henry), no one who read "The Beast in the Dingle" in the late 1940's could doubt. But the actual extent of his familiarity with this progressively impenetrable jungle Thurber waited until 1959 to demonstrate formally. This he did in "The Wings of Henry James," a striking performance on several counts, and not all of them predictable. "The Wings" is a long piece that starts out as a study of James's *The Wings of the Dove* and, as it meanders in its inimitably mazy motion, courses through the vast James continent and reveals not only an acquaintance with James's *Wings* dating back to World War I, when he took a course in the modern novel in his University Days at Ohio State, but a bibliophilic and bibliographic—not to speak of psychoanalytic—knowledge of Henry James as impressive as that of his plots and effects.

How much else—I found myself, for all the world like one of James's own fictional devotees, wondering—had he done with James? Possibly enough to warrant a collection for the entertainment and edification of us Jamesians? I asked him in a letter in the summer of 1961 (the last of his life). He put me off with characteristic modesty, confessing that although he was grateful for my interest, he had written only "four pieces" about Henry James: "One was an early casual in *The New Yorker,* and another, probably the best known in academic circles [such as my letter head betrayed mine to be], a pastiche called 'The Beast in the Dingle.' I don't believe that it adds up to a collectable group. . . ."

That "early casual," I supposed, a search of *New Yorker* files might turn up. Then (subtracting the obvious and recent "Wings"

article that had prompted my inquiry) what was the fourth, that
Thurber couldn't identify even as casually as he did that "early
casual"? I was just challenged enough to try to find out, and in the
intervening two years and more have done enough leg (as well as
seat-of-the-pants) work to find out that although his contributions
to Jamesiana *don't* add up to a collectable group, Thurber's memory was fallible: that count of "four" was far short. Exactly *how* far,
I leave to what Thurber called "some strong young literary execu-
tor" to determine. For the present I would like merely to report on
a few excavations of my own. They are not the familiar, recognizable, and accessible Thurber-on-James pieces.[1] Rather, they are five
or six still other, fairly unfamiliar ones (not to speak of at least that
many fragments, odds and ends—one or two of which I have already
made use of in Chapter One, above, that Thurber did not see fit to
reprint—could not, it would appear, even remember). From these
alone it is possible to draw at least two conclusions: One is that
Henry James figures far more prominently in James Thurber's own
works than the modest disclaimer of his letter first gave me to believe; another, that James Thurber is a far more sensitive admirer
of the indefinable qualities which people admire in Henry James
fiction as well as a devastating satirist (that is, critic) of the qualities
we regret in it, than he has yet been given credit for.

The Wings of the Dove may have been the James that Thurber
recalled in *his* "Wings" from that course in the modern English
novel, but the truly lasting effects of Professor Joseph Russell Taylor's patient evangelizing, Thurber had disclosed parenthetically
earlier in "The First Time I Saw Paris." For here we discover that
it was through no less original a window than James's *Ambassadors*
that young Thurber did his seeing in anticipation when, in November, 1918, he debarked at Saint-Nazaire in his first trip abroad. (The
third of the late James trio, *The Golden Bowl*, was quite another
story, as we shall see.) His youthful excitement revives for us in this
thirty-year-old reminiscence of his approach to the fabulous city to
which, Thurber possibly already knew—from James's "International Episode," if not from its original source—all good Americans
ordinarily went only when they died: "The train trip down to Paris
was a night to remember. . . . I lay awake a long time thinking of
the only Paris I knew, the tranquil, almost somnolent city of Henry

[1] "The Beast in the Dingle" is reprinted in *The Beast in Me and Other Animals,* New York, 1948; "The Wings of Henry James," in *Lanterns and Lances,*
New York, 1961.

James's turn-of-the-century novels, in which there was no hint of war, past or present, except that of the sexes." [2]

This reminiscence I find noteworthy in several ways. First, considering that—as Thurber himself pointed out in his "Wings"—it was not until the 1940's that the Henry James Revival took place; that, at the time Thurber is recalling, James had been dead only two years and had died unread, unmourned, and—partly because of the state of the world in 1916—practically unnoticed;[3] that at this time if romantic young Americans envisioned Paris through the window of art, it was Du Maurier's Paris, or Dumas's, or Hugo's, or Puccini's or Zola's; in view of all these factors, this 1918 conversion to Henry James must be one of the earliest on record of the many following James's death.

Secondly, there is the phrase "war . . . of the sexes." I think that it would be worth the while of some other ponderer of literary relationships to determine the extent to which the massive, menacing, tyrannical females of line drawing and short story in James Thurber's long and voluminous career are inspired by The Henry James Female. "*She* is of the strenuous pattern"—could not James Thurber have described, say, Miss Ulgine Barrows of "The Catbird Seat" as exactly by the phrase that The Master had used in his Notebooks in projecting Mrs. Newsome of *The Ambassadors*? Or Kate Croy in *The Wings of the Dove*? Austin Warren has called to our notice the metaphors with which James's male characters frequently conceive such females:[4] Mrs. Lowder, as seen through Merton Densher's eyes in *The Golden Bowl*, is encased in armor; is a steamboat steering an imperious course; is "a projectile, of great size, loaded and ready for use." Even the barely seen Mrs. Midmore of *The Sense of the Past* and the completely unseen Mrs. Newsome of *The Ambassadors* are, Professor Warren continues, "women as massive as, ultimately, men-

---

2 "The First Time I Saw Paris," *Holiday*, XXI (April, 1957). Reprinted in *Alarms and Diversions*, New York, 1957.

3 Around this time, too, Heywood Broun recalled, in response to his order from Switzerland for James's *The Better Sort* (1903), "One [London] bookshop replied that Mr. James had never written a book of that title, another that it was then in the process of being published—[while in truth] it had been out some five or six years. . . ." (*The Turn of the Screw*, Modern Library [1930], Introduction.)

4 Actually, even the James females are capable of looking upon other females with this trepidation. Witness the repeated metaphors of *enormousness*, of immensity, and their companion of *might* in which the morbidly fearful Adela Chart of "The Marriages" conceives Mrs. Churchley: when the maid announces " 'a lady,' " Adela, mistakenly thinking it Mrs. Churchley, asks " 'Is she big and dreadful?' "

acing. . . ." [5] Correspondingly, Thurber's Mr. Mittys and Mr. Martins and the "poor sensitive gentlemen" of James's "attested predilection" seem to beg for a similar identification. . . .

I should also offer the reminder, however, that that sex-war-oriented commentary on *The Ambassadors* is as misleading as it is thought-provoking; for no matter what his later contemplations or readings of that novel may have inspired, James Thurber's first meeting with the Countess was a case of love at first sight. This he declared in various ways and over a long period of time. In the Mood Critical-Autobiographical-Historical, we find his remarks to Mark Van Doren and Lyman Bryson in the symposium "Henry James: *The Ambassadors.*" Here he maintains that *The Ambassadors* "isn't tedious . . . if you are on all three or four levels of appreciation when reading it. But for that, I admit, you have to be a Henry James man. I happen to be one, and this is one of my favorite books. I have read it four times in the last thirty-five years." [6] He catches Mr. Van Doren in an error of fact (it was the scenario, not the manuscript, of *The Ambassadors* that the reader for *Harper's* rejected in 1903; and for publication as a serial in *Harper's* magazine, not as a book under the Harper imprint); and anticipating his vast knowledge of Jamesiana in the 1959 "The Wings," goes on to list various James fictions that "became popular in other people's hands," ending with the reminder that *The Ambassadors* had been done twice on television and once on radio. . . .

But more than all else, there is the Mood Mellow and Romantic. Going back to the 1951–1952 symposium, we find Thurber recollecting that Ohio State University professor Joseph Russell Taylor had said that in this same Mme. de Vionnet "Henry James has created a woman of great charm, whose activity in the novel is charm, and charm is a very hard thing to have, or to write about"; and that apropos Strether's final support of the lovers even after he learns that their relationship is carnal, Strether "has this line that Professor Taylor used to print and that I've often used in stories: 'When she touches a thing, the ugliness, God knows how, goes out of it.' [7] Taylor used to say that that is as fine a definition of charm in a woman as has been written." [8]

Now it is an easy step from here to an episode *not* included in

---

[5] "Myth and Dialectic in the Later Novels," 560.

[6] *Invitation to Learning*, I (Winter, 1952), 355–366.

[7] "As she presented things the ugliness—goodness knew why—went out of them. . . ." (*The Ambassadors*, Book Twelfth.)

[8] *Invitation to Learning*, I, 367.

"The Secret Life of James Thurber," and, if reprinted in book form not once but twice,[9] yet under the cover of a title ("A Call on Mrs. Forrester") that will throw off the scent all but the genuine "Henry James man," who will find hidden underneath: "After rereading, in my middle years, Willa Cather's 'A Lost Lady' and Henry James's 'The Ambassadors.' "[10] In this charming 1948 phantasy the narrator is palpably an American Lambert Strether, as all of the blatant mockery, and Walter Mitty-like practicality are powerless to conceal from the reader. Like James's middle-aged hero at the end of *The Ambassadors,* Thurber-Strether, on a call to Marian Forrester in Burlington after fifteen years, "wondered, standing there in the rain, how it would all come out." [11] He thinks of himself as waxing eloquent with brandy and betraying to one lost lady his secret attachment to another: "I would then confess my love for Madame de Vionnet, the lady of the lilacs, of Gloriani's bright Sunday garden, of the stately house in the Boulevard Malesherbes, with its cool parlor and dark medallions." (Yet it closes with the no-nonsense voice of admonishment of an invisible Mrs. Mitty-Newsome: "A man's a fool who walks in the rain. . . . Besides, if you miss the 6:15 . . . , you have to wait till midnight for the next train east. A man could catch his death, dozing there in that cold and lonesome station.")

But to get back. In the above charming bit of whimsy, written well along in Thurber's career, there is a distinguishably Jamesian note. But it is one that Thurber had struck long years before in his relationship with Henry James—in, as a matter of fact, the first serious venture into The Master's jungle that Thurber ever made (so far as either of us has been able to discover). This is one that appeared in the January 11, 1930, issue of *The New Yorker* as apparently merely another in a series of slight satiric sketches featuring one John Monroe. Its title, "The Middle Years," promises a link with James's story of the same name that the story itself fulfills; for Thurber's is in a random sort of way an imitation of James's. . . .

There is even this thrust at James's usual unwillingness to give sex a respectable hearing: "He would begin the communion on a ma-

9 In *The Beast in Me and Other Animals,* and *Alarms and Diversions.*

10 That equally early Henry James Man, Edmund Wilson, had associated *A Lost Lady* with Henry James as soon as she raised her wistful head, but only to identify the technique of the novel with James's "indirect method," the "Jamesian glass" Cather uses to show us her heroine by—namely, the various "limpid and sensitive young men" of her story. (See *The Shores of Light,* p. 42.)

11 "He remembered everything, . . . falling back above all on the great interests of [his and Maria's] early time, the curiosity felt by both of them as to where he would 'come out.' " (*The Ambassadors,* Book Twelfth.)

ture, a 'wonderful' plane. . . . [Then] it crossed his mind that the
lady might have other patterns in mind than those of Henry James."
Finally, even verbal echoes of The Master are faintly audible. Monroe's final, deep sigh could be any one of "poor" Dencombe's many,
and Thurber's description of Monroe's response to the invitation
to intrigue ("He merely favored her with an intense and wonderful
glance . . .") sounds like something lifted entire from James's own
work. And it is an amused mockery that runs through Thurber. In
the much later piece we find him writing: "I was upon it in a moment, hastily assuming my best Henry James garden-party manner.
'How perfectly charming of them both, dear lady,' I wonderfully
cried." [12] Again, in a quite serious manner, in the symposium on
The Ambassadors, when commenting on the phrase "intensely
there" from the early Wells lampoon on James, Thurber pleads:
"Well, 'intensely there' is, of course, one of the finest two words ever
written. 'Intensely there' is right, in his purposes and everything
else. . . ." [13]

Yet, if this is little to say of a James story these days, even less can
be said of the next James story that Thurber drew on for a lampoon,
a *New Yorker* profile of July 30, 1932, entitled "Something to Say."
Certainly "The Coxon Fund," in whose light it must be seen, is so
distended and flaccid a production that, to my knowledge, no one
has seen fit to reprint it since its appearance in the New York and
London editions of James's works.

[12] "Party of One: Such a Phrase as Drifts Through Dreams," *Holiday*, XXVIII
(Dec., 1960). Reprinted in *Lanterns and Lances*.

[13] This same mixture, or alternation, of annoyance and admiration with respect
to James's style can be found very early in Thurber's *New Yorker* pieces. In an
article (one of a series entitled "Our Own Modern English Usage") on "Which"
appearing on May 4, 1929, Thurber wrote that "Not even Henry James could have
successfully emerged from a sentence with 'which,' 'whom,' and 'being' in it."
And in a much longer piece ("Isn't Life Lovely!") of June 25, 1932, an out-and-
out *jeu d'esprit*, Thurber rewrites Ford Madox Ford's *Return to Yesterday* as
Elsie Janis would have written it. In this imitation Thurber includes a good deal
of reminiscence of Henry James (whom Ford knew well). The only part of this
nonsensical drollery to our point concerns James's style: "Mr. James was adorably
funny. He began in the middle of a sentence and spoke both ways at once, reaching the beginning and the end of what he was trying to say at the same time.
'He appears to be getting some place but he is really going nowhere, with his hat
and coat on backwards,' Crane said."

And in a piece for *Punch* ("The New Vocabularianism," reprinted in *Lanterns
and Lances*): "A sensitive gentleman in one of Henry James's novels exclaims at
the end, triumphantly, 'Then there we are!' not because he and his fair companion have arrived at a solution of anything but because they have come upon
an embraceable impasse."

Beginning, as James later recalled, with the idea of the brilliant
talker Coleridge as Campbell's books suggested it to him, James
presented here one Frank Saltram in a parable of the life of the
mind. Saltram is an egregious, lovable and infuriating genius-ass. He
dresses outlandishly, keeps dinner waiting, comes down as a guest so
late for breakfast that cook after cook has quit in protest; "drinks
like a fish"; fails to keep speaking engagements that admirers have
generously arranged; is indifferent to the fate of his wife and lawful
children (not to speak of three bastards sired earlier); and repays his
generous and long-suffering sponsors and hosts with the coin of wit
and aphorism rather than the written or publicly delivered word.
James ends this story suddenly and patently ironically, by having a
financial windfall (the Coxon Fund) prove Saltram's actual ruin:
"Its magnificence . . . quite quenched him; it was the beginning of
his decline. . . . The very day he found himself able to publish he
wholly ceased to produce," leaving the narrator to reflect mourn-
fully that "we were all happier as well as poorer before. . . ."

It is from this trying person that the central figure of Thurber's
"Something to Say" originates. . . . Thurber's brilliant talker bears
the name Elliot Vereker. It happens that the surname of this cad is
borrowed from an equally difficult man of letters from yet another
James story (included in the same volume of the New York and
London editions that contains "The Coxon Fund"), "The Figure
in the Carpet." Its Hugh Vereker is an equally trying (but prolific)
writer. Still other parallels with "The Figure in the Carpet" can be
cited, as curious as they are individually inconsequential. One is
James's Drayton Deane, a literary critic who reappears in a minor
passage as Thurber's literary critic Marvin Deane. In an even less
important context there are James's Miss Poyle, identified as "the
vicar's sister," and Thurber's talker's penchant for using four-letter
words "when he was talking to a little child or the sister of a vicar." [14]

But it is "The Coxon Fund" that is Thurber's main model, beyond any doubt. His Elliot Vereker is not so much a travesty of
Frank Saltram as he is a consistent and logical extension of him.
Now, in the original, James's narrator is generally able to maintain
an objectivity toward Saltram—a moral distaste and esthetic delight
simultaneously existing—that permits Saltram's boorishness and

---

[14] Could it be that Miss Poyle could not help reappearing, even if anonymously,
because Thurber had remembered James's characterization of her as "a robust
unmodulated person" who is capable of "thrust[ing] her chin half[way] across the
cloth" of the dinner table?

charm to vie with one another (a method of characterization that Austin Warren terms "dialectic"—that is, definition by thesis, antithesis, and synthesis). . . . Yet James's very idea is subject to a double jeopardy in the working out. For not only is it not really possible to convey the effect of Saltram's presence—an ineffable combination of charm and luminousness—merely, as James tries to do, by repeating his assertion that it exists and works: it is, conversely, all too easy to convey the sense of Saltram's oafishness simply by citing instances from his personal actions. And the quality of the man that remains imprinted in the reader's awareness is, unfortunately, this very oafishness, for it is demonstrated at the story's every turn.

Now it is precisely this quality that Thurber not only restricts himself to but, appositely enough, develops by copious illustration. His Elliot Vereker is a thoroughgoing poseur. He effects outlandish traits. He has "no reverence and no solicitude," is a wantonly destructive houseguest. His literary work is all of the abortive variety ("His entire output . . . consisted of only twenty or thirty pages, most of them bearing the round stain of liquor glasses. . . ."), but "His was the true, artistic fire, the rare gesture of genius . . . ," and all of his friends feel that he is "one of the great original minds of our generation. That he had 'something to say' was obvious in everything he did. . . ."

Yet even if one contends that Vereker is simply a parody, a violation, of the James original, Thurber still must be seen as barely, if at all, concerning himself with the aspect of the Saltram story that gives James's story what little claim it has to a reader's attention. I refer to the complexity of the relationships that form and re-form among the various Saltram admirers, dependents, and sponsors, victims and champions, as a result of the talker's capricious antics. These are as implausibly complex and motivated as those that result from the original Vereker's equally mystifying conduct in James's companion piece, "The Figure in the Carpet." And this, Thurber never touches, restricting himself to the more naturally burlesque-able antics of Saltram himself. This was, inherently, the weak part of James's story, and Thurber demolished it hilariously.

But seventeen years later, as though returning to business left unfinished, Thurber wrote a piece whose subtitle announces its composition as resulting from ". . . Reading Two or Three Literary Memorials, To This or That Lamented Talent, Written By One Critic or Another," and whose title is "A Final Note on Chanda

Bell," [15] but whose substance is a burlesque of Henry James's "The Figure in the Carpet," for all that. There James had implausibly set in motion a group of characters who put aside all other concerns in life in order to discover the meaning underlying the clever but ostensibly superficial novels of Hugh Vereker. . . .

Never had Henry James written anything to such an airy thinness beat, had he carried to such absurd extremes the sacrifices to which a basically silly proposition would carry people, even the hypercurious. For the reader, the fatal weakness of the story is that if its Vereker has not made his underlying theme apparent even to the initiate after twenty volumes, it is not possible that the theme is an idea at all; whereas if, on the other hand, the underlying theme is not an idea but simply a device or trick,—that is, literally a *figure*, —then it is not possible for any person of normal character to concern himself about it for any great length of time. . . .

Thurber explodes this concatenation of absurdities with an instrument perfect for the provocation—silliness. His cryptic author is an aging woman who, like Vereker, both invites the narrator[16] and teases him to guess the meaning of her fiction: " 'You have found the figure, . . .' she told me one afternoon, 'but have you found the carpet?' "

> *A year of my friendship with the gifted lady had passed . . . before I could be sure that I knew what she was trying not to say. . . . Her use of the triple negative, in such expressions as "not unmeaningless," and her habit of starting sentences in the middle bewildered [Vayne], and so did her fondness for surrogate words with ambiguous meanings, like the words in dreams: "rupture" for "rapture," "centaur" for "sender," "pressure" for "pleasure," and "scorpio" for "scrofula." She enjoyed frustrating him, and she made the most of his discomfiture.*

Thurber's narrator is also incredibly curious, indefatigable, and worshipful. It is true that as time passes he suffers disenchantment, but this is only fitful. His suspicion that Chanda is not so much a mystery as a hoax does not keep him from such valiant efforts at deciphering her as reading one of her books backward and upside down—an undertaking that leaves him unable to tell "whether it was beauty or balderdash." After her death, he confronts her one

---

[15] *The New Yorker*, XXV (October 15, 1949). Reprinted in *Thurber Country*, New York, 1953.

[16] In both James's and Thurber's stories, the narrator is someone who has written an understanding review of the author for the public press.

intimate, the butler Hadley, with a demand for the meaning of her mystery (" 'What is the carpet?' I shouted"), only to be told, " 'I do not know what you mean.' " (" 'I don't know what you're talking about,' " Gwendolyn's second husband had told James's equally outraged narrator.) And whereas, unlike him, Thurber's critic lives in mortal fear that in some posthumous manuscript Chanda Bell will expose "her stuff as the merest junk" (and his own "penetrating analysis" of it, therefore, "as a monument to a fatuous gullibility"), still he ends his narration with a renewed demonstration of that gullibility (possibly, of dawning common sense?): "Meanwhile, I have hit on a new approach to the works of Chanda Bell. I am trying to read them sideways."

The excessive speed with which time was, even in the 1930's, making up for its neglect of Henry James is the provocation for Thurber's "early casual," which I herewith identify as his "Recollections of Henry James" of *The New Yorker* for June 17, 1933. This begins as an expression of annoyance that "In almost every autobiography that I have picked up in the past four or five years, there has been a chapter devoted to reminiscences and impressions of Henry James." He lists those not only by such plausibles as Gertrude Atherton, W. H. Hudson, Ezra Pound, and Hugh Walpole, but others by Ambrose Bierce, Gene Tunney, and *um Gotteswillen* "Doug and Mary Fairbanks." This kind of tomfoolery distinguishes the *jeu d'esprit* that is the greater part of Thurber's piece, in which he imagines an afternoon in the past when Henry James was telling— actually *not* telling—the plot of a current hit, "The Bat. . . ."

But James Thurber could write yet another form of criticism of Henry James than the one that subtle imitations or sentimental or ludicrous farces constitute. He was capable on occasion of formal insights worthy of serious consideration. Evidence of this aspect of Thurber's relationship to James is less frequent and less striking but is in its way possibly the most impressive of all, intellectually speaking, for it reveals the true range of Thurber's mind. It appears unexpectedly in the context of a review of Eugene O'Neill's *Days Without End* that Thurber wrote for *The New Yorker* of January 20, 1934, entitled "One Man in His Time." Here Thurber relates the technical virtuosity of the dramatist to the innovation of the earlier novelist:

> One of my speculations has been about a certain similarity between Mr. O'Neill's devices in the drama and Henry James's strategies in his later novels. They have at least one thing in common—an "indirectness of narrative technique," as Ludwig Lewi-

sohn has called it. Had Mr. James lived another ten years, he
might conceivably have got so far away from direct narration that
instead of simply telling what occurred when two persons came
together, he would have presented it through the consciousness of
a Worcester, Massachusetts, lawyer who got it from the proprietor
of a café who had overheard two people at a table piecing together a story they had listened in on at a large and crowded
party. The difference between the indirectness of James and that
of O'Neill lies in the fact that whereas James got farther and
farther away from his central character by filtering that central
character through the perceptions of other people, O'Neill achieves
his remoteness of contact by having his central character get
farther and farther away from himself through splitting up into
various phases of viewpoint and behavior.

But Thurber's most sustained venture into criticism of James
(which also resulted from his duties as a play reviewer), to my knowledge, is also one of his most unfamiliar pieces of writing. . . . The
occasion was the New York opening of the play by John L. Balderston,[17] *Berkeley Square*; almost the first of Thurber's ventures into
James was his brief but knowing review of that play entitled "A
Popular Hit and Its Debt to a Novelist." This is to be found in the
New York Tribune for February 2, 1930. . . .

First, a paragraph or two of acknowledgments. The play having
been modeled on a ghost story of James's, Thurber went unerringly
to James's own pronouncement on this genre in his preface to the
Altar of the Dead volume:

> The peril of the unmeasured strange, in fiction, [is] the silly,
> just as its strength . . . is charming. . . . The ideal . . . is the
> straight fairy tale. . . . It may seem odd, in search of the amusing,
> to try to steer wide of the silly by hugging close to the "supernat-
> ural"; but . . . "the ghost story" . . . has ever been for me the
> most possible form of the fairy tale.

The Master, Thurber reminded his readers, was a story-teller, not
a Thinker: "The notion seems to exist that the authors merely borrowed James's 'general idea of metaphysics'—I heard it so described
one night at the play—between acts. Henry James, of course, didn't
give a hang about metaphysics as such." James, he insisted, "saw no
danger in being 'wrong' in any scientific sense—but only in being
'silly.' . . ."

Now, although Henry James had no interest in metaphysics—in

[17] With the "invaluable assistance of J. C. Squire."

ideas in the philosophical sense of that word, as Thurber (and T. S. Eliot before him) had pointed out, what he personally had at all times and what interpenetrated his entire literary production was a love of the past beyond telling. And here in just this regard was *Berkeley Square*'s chief offense against the spirit of Henry James. For James to send his young man from 1910 back into 1820 was one thing; for Balderston, back 140 years or more, quite another, actually. For, as Thurber pointed out—again going for his evidence to a James preface, this time to the *Aspern Papers* volume—to James the only past to be visited, whether in phantasy or reality, was the *just vanishing* past: this alone could actually be experienced.

> I delight in a palpable imaginable visitable past—in the nearer distances and the clearer mysteries, the . . . world we may reach over to as by making a long arm we grasp an object at the other end of our own table. . . . That, to my imagination, is the past fragrant of all, or almost all, the poetry of the thing outlived and lost and gone. . . . With more moves back the element of the appreciable shrinks. . . . —the view is mainly a view of barriers. . . . It would take me too far . . . to tell why the particular afternoon light that I thus call intense rests clearer to my sense on the Byronic age . . . than on the periods more protected by the "dignity" of history. With the times beyond, intrinsically more "strange," the tender grace, for the backward vision, has faded, the afternoon darkened; for any time nearer to us the special effect hasn't begun.

In that passage, cited at a time when, except as the author of *Daisy Miller* and of that *earlier* ghost story, "The Turn of the Screw," Henry James was largely unknown to the American public, Thurber had singled out what is now generally taken as possibly James's most valuable insight into his person and his art. Adding this insight of Thurber's to the one that concludes his "Recollections of Henry James," and these, in turn, to his numerous other, far-ranging comments, we realize that, prank-playing, mockery and all, one of the earliest and always one of the most reliable of the many guides to the solemn, formidable Master in this country was James Thurber.

PART TWO

The Individual Talent: Early and Middle Years

Unbaked Cookies

by Dorothy Parker

Once a friend of a friend of mine was riding a London bus. At her stop she came down the stair just behind two ladies who, even during descent, were deep in conversation; surely only the discussion of the shortcomings of a common acquaintance could have held them so absorbed. She heeded their voices but none of their words, until the lady in advance stopped on a step, turned and declaimed in melodious British: "Mad, I don't say. Queer, I grant you. Many's the time I've seen her nude at the piano."

It has been, says this friend of my friend's, the regret of her days that she did not hear what led up to that strange fragment of biography.

But there I stray from her. It is infinitely provocative, I think, to be given only the climax; infinitely beguiling to wander back from it along the dappled paths of fancy. The words of that lady of the bus have all the challenge of a Thurber drawing—indeed, I am practically convinced that she herself *was* a Thurber drawing. No one but Mr. Thurber could have thought of her.

Mr. James Thurber, our hero, deals solely in culminations. Beneath his pictures he sets only the final line. You may figure for yourself, and good luck to you, what under heaven could have gone before, that his sombre citizens find themselves in such remarkable situations. It is yours to ponder how penguins get into drawing-rooms and seals into bed-chambers, for Mr. Thurber will only show them to you some little time after they have arrived there. Superbly he slaps aside preliminaries. He gives you a glimpse of the startling present and lets you go construct the astounding past. And if, somewhere in that process, you part with a certain amount of sanity, doubtless you are better off without it. There is too much sense in this world anyway.

"Unbaked Cookies" (editor's title). From Dorothy Parker, "Introduction" in James Thurber, *The Seal in the Bedroom and Other Predicaments* (New York: Harper & Row, Publishers, Inc., 1932). Copyright 1932 by James Thurber. Reprinted by permission of the publisher.

These are strange people that Mr. Thurber has turned loose upon us. They seem to fall into three classes—the playful, the defeated, and the ferocious. All of them have the outer semblance of unbaked cookies; the women are of a dowdiness so overwhelming that it becomes tremendous style. Once a heckler, who should have been immediately put out, complained that the Thurber women have no sex appeal. The artist was no more than reproachful. "They have for my men," he said. And certainly the Thurber men, those deplorably *desoigne* Thurber men, would ask no better.

There is about all these characters, even the angry ones, a touching quality. They expect so little of life; they remember the old discouragements and await the new. They are not shrewd people, nor even bright, and we must all be very patient with them. Lambs in a world of wolves, they are, and there is on them a protracted innocence. One sees them daily, come alive from the pages of *The New Yorker*—sees them in trains and ferryboats and station waiting-rooms and all the big, sad places where a face is once beheld, never to be seen again. It is curious, perhaps terrible, how Mr. Thurber has influenced the American face and physique, and some day he will surely answer for it. People didn't go about looking like that before he started drawing. But now there are more and more of them doing it, all the time. Presently, it may be, we shall become a nation of Thurber drawings, and then the Japanese can come over and lick the tar out of us.

Of the birds and animals so bewilderingly woven into the lives of the Thurber people it is best to say but little. Those tender puppies, those faint-hearted hounds—I think they are hounds—that despondent penguin—one goes all weak with sentiment. No man could have drawn, much less thought of, those creatures unless he felt really right about animals. One gathers that Mr. Thurber does, his art aside; he has fourteen resident dogs and more are expected. Reason totters.

All of them, his birds and his beasts and his men and women, are actually dashed off by the artist. Ten minutes for a drawing he regards as drudgery. He draws with a pen, with no foundation of pencil, and so sure and great is his draughtsmanship that there is never a hesitating line, never a change. No one understands how he makes his boneless, loppy beings, with their shy kinship to the men and women of Picasso's later drawings, so truly and gratifyingly decorative. And no one, with the exception of God and possibly Mr. Thurber, knows from what dark breeding-ground come the artist's ideas. Analysis promptly curls up; how is one to shadow the mental processes of a man who is impelled to depict a seal looking over the headboard of a bed occupied by a broken-spirited husband and a virago of a wife, and then to write below the scene the one line "All right, have it your way—you heard a seal bark"? . . . Mad, I don't say. Genius, I grant you.

It is none too soon that Mr. Thurber's drawings have been assembled in one space. Always one wants to show an understanding friend a conceit that the artist published in *The New Yorker*—let's see, how many weeks ago was it? and always some other understanding friend has been there first and sneaked the back copies of the magazine home with him. And it is necessary really to show the picture. A Thurber must be seen to be believed—there is no use trying to tell the plot of it. Only one thing is more hopeless than attempting to describe a Thurber drawing, and that is trying not to tell about it. So everything is going to be much better, I know, now that all the pictures are here together. Perhaps the one constructive thing in this year of hell is the publication of this collection.

And it is my pleasure and privilege—though also, I am afraid, my presumption—to introduce to you, now, one you know well already; one I revere as an artist and cleave to as a friend. Ladies and gentlemen—Mr. James Thurber.

The Icon and the Portrait

by W. H. Auden

There has always been a competition in the visual arts between iconography and portraiture, the symbolic and the unique, the God and the mortal. In the great periods of Italian and German art, that is, up to the middle of the sixteenth century, these two elements coexisted in a fruitful tension and equilibrium. Not only was it possible, for instance, to use realistic portraits of models for icons in religious pictures, but also the relation of man to the rest of nature, of the spiritual to the temporal was never in doubt; witness the elaborate and significant, almost surrealist landscapes in such painting.

For a whole complex of reasons, psychological, political, and economic, this equilibrium was destroyed. The main current of painting confined itself more and more to portraiture, whether of people or still life, and iconography was relegated to the cartoon, which, the genius of Goya and Daumier notwithstanding, wore a slightly disreputable air, as if it had to apologize for not being noble or serious.

In recent years, however, iconography has begun to recover its prestige; the interest in child art, Negro sculpture, and doodling, the popularity of Disney and Thurber are evidences of this. Yet a synthesis of icon and portrait is still far off. The former remains non-representational, the latter accidental. It would be as impertinent as it is unnecessary for me to praise Mr. Thurber's work; everyone knows and loves it. All I can do is to point out what I believe to be certain deficiencies common both to him as an artist and to us all as people.

The spiritual father of the tradition to which both Mr. Thurber and Mr. Steig belong is Edward Lear, that remarkable artist who supplemented what he thought of as his serious work, his realistic

"The Icon and the Portrait" by W. H. Auden. From *The Nation,* CL (January 13, 1940), 48. Copyright 1940 by *The Nation.* Reprinted by permission of *The Nation.*

pre-Raphaelite landscapes, with scribbled diagrams of his inner life.
To Lear as to Thurber after him, the icon is the average non-political man of an industrialized society—who is surprisingly the same in Park Avenue and the Bowery—the person who in large enough numbers makes up what the damned refer to as the Masses. The popularity of their work with all classes indicates that such an icon is a valid one for our present stage of culture.

Is it not, then, a little disconcerting to find how little of life has today any iconographic significance, that is, seems both universal and capable of inspiring reverence and love? Not only landscape but the human figure itself has to be reduced to the barest outline—even sexual differences almost disappear. All detail, all portraiture belong to the world of the enemy, those unpleasant and powerful forces which Lear called "They" and Thurber calls the Liberators, the world whose art is the realistic bosh of society portraits and statues representing the workers of tomorrow. The realm of modern freedom is indeed limited.

"The Last Flower" is a parable about social life. Their amenities destroyed by war, deserted even by their dogs, down to their last flower, a young man and woman rediscover sex; society is rebuilt; back come the dogs and the politicians and war; and the cycle begins all over again. This is at once both too pessimistic and not pessimistic enough. It suggests (1) that all politicians are equally evil, and (2) that all lovers are without error. But the public and the private life are not so distinct. If all politicians do evil, yet no lover is innocent, and there are better and worse politicians just as there are better and worse lovers. Mr. Thurber's heresy is particularly dangerous because it flatters our conceit; every reader will call the lovers Me and My Girl, while he will equally naturally call the Liberators Mr. R or Mr. H.

This is where Mr. Steig comes in. When Mr. Thurber has debunked the Liberators, Mr. Steig carries on by debunking the lovers. If "About People" makes others as uncomfortable as it makes me, I'm afraid Mr. Steig will not become widely popular; for he is unequivocally pessimistic: the only virtue he grants the human species is a capacity to perceive and laugh at its folly. Though this is, I believe, too negative to be an adequate response to life—a sense of humor is rarely without an element of fear—it is an indispensable preliminary. We shall never earn the right to lift our heads till we have learned to hang them.

Nor is it, I hope, merely fanciful, to connect this politico-ethical problem of our thinking and conduct with the artistic problem of how to combine the icon and the portrait. Just as we have still to discover the proper relations of the private and public life, so the inward-looking artist has to unlearn his puritanical distrust of matter, and the outward-looking his crude faith in the kingdoms of this world. Logos and Eros have yet to be reconciled in a new Agape.

New Yorker Days

by Robert M. Coates

James Thurber, in his *The Years with Ross*, has described how, one day in 1927, he went up to the offices of the *New Yorker* to discuss, as he thought, the possible purchase of some pieces he had sent in to the magazine, and found himself instead—and considerably to his dismay—hired on the spot as its managing editor. That was Ross's way at the time. Similarly, I went up there a couple of years later, as I thought to discuss a couple of pieces I had sent in, hopefully; was interviewed by Thurber, and found myself taken on instead to work, along with Jim himself and E. B. White, on the department called "Talk Of The Town."

By then, to his relief, Jim had succeeded in getting himself demoted from his original exalted position. It was a job he had never wanted in the first place. From his earliest days, he had wanted to be a writer; nothing else would do, and a writer he remained preeminently, in spite of all his other accomplishments, to the end—and about as dedicated a one as I have ever seen.

But he prided himself on his ability as a reporter, too. Before coming to the *New Yorker*, he had worked for a while on the old New York Evening Post, and before that, during his years abroad, on the Paris edition of the *New York Herald*.[1] As a working newspaperman he had, by his own admission, his errant side. (He liked to tell of the time he was sent to cover a fire in Brooklyn, and came back to say that he hadn't been able to find it—and would go on to describe the look on his city editor's face as he digested the announcement. "A four alarm fire," Jim quoted the poor man as saying, "and this fellow just can't find it!")

Talk Of The Town, however, or as we called it, more simply, Talk—less hidebound, less "who-what-when-where-why" conscious

"New Yorker Days" (editor's title). From Robert M. Coates, "James Thurber," *Authors Guild Bulletin* (December 1961). Copyright © 1961 by The Authors League of America, Inc. Reprinted by permission of Harold Ober Associates Incorporated.

1 [Actually the Paris edition of the *Chicago Tribune*—Ed.]

than the dailies—was just made for him, as he was made for it, and it is no more than simple fact to say that he "made" the department too, into its present image. He worked full time on it, I worked only part time. Andy White, more and more, as time went on, devoted himself to the writing of those more or less straight "editorial" paragraphs, impeccable in style, on the lead-off "Notes and Comment" page.

The department, then—indeed, the whole magazine—was in what could hardly be called with more reason its "formative" stage. I'm sure that Andy White would agree that it was Thurber, more than anyone else, who reached out, captured, and molded into reality Ross's inchoate dream of what Talk should be. It wasn't an easy task, I realize now. A good, crisp writing style, mingling the essayistic deceptively with the reportorial, was required, first of all. Jim had that. Unfailing good taste was needed too, for the air of casualness we affected could easily have been led off into mere whimsicality. (I still remember how depressed we used to be when would-be contributors would send in anecdotes or other items couched in a kind of pseudo-British, high-toned jargon: the very thing we were trying to avoid.) A respect for simple accuracy was needed too, for the same reason, as well as an instinct for the central interest in a given story.

Jim had these attributes, for despite his occasional lapses in bemusement when confronted with routine newspaper assignments, he was a good reporter. Perhaps the best, the most beautiful thing the job offered—remember that in those days Jim was still a young man from Ohio—was the fact that it gave him the whole wonderful city of New York to ramble about in, explore, study, and write about. . . .

I'd still like to come back to the early days. Thurber's total accomplishments were many, indeed. Yet like many a man of wide achievements, he took perhaps his greater pride in what may seem to be lesser talents. He was a Civil War buff long before that became fashionable, and a baseball fan of equally impressive stature: he knew the history of even the minor Civil War skirmishes, particularly those that occurred around Southern Ohio—including some that have largely gone unnoticed by the more heavy-gauged historals; while he could, at the drop of a hat, give you the Earned Run Averages of every big league pitcher back to Christy Mathewson, and the RBI, HH totals and yearly batting averages of practically every player on down from Ty Cobb and Honus Wagner.

At the drop of a hat, too, till his eyes failed, if the hat had been dropped brim-side up in the center of the room—like, for instance, the living room of Jap and Helen Gude, or others of his lifelong friends—he would proudly display his ability to flip more cards, out of a deck of playing cards, than any other contestant, into the said hat. It was an accomplishment that I always thought—perhaps because I usually ranked low in it—had its lucky side. It was a messy game, too, necessitating a lot of scrambling around to re-assemble the cards and it usually ended up with the deck rumpled and ruined. But it was his pride.

He was proud, too, of his repertoire of old ballads ("Bye, Bye, Blackbird," "Stormy Weather," "Melancholy Baby" and so on) as he was of his prowess at the word games ("Guggenheim," Anagrams, and so on) that we all played so indefatigably, evenings, in those innocent, early days. I think, too, that in some ways he was proudest of all of his exploits in the old "Talk" days, when, after briefly studying some anecdote or other small item that had been sent in to us, he would put it down beside his typewriter in the jammed-up little office we happily shared and proceed to rewrite it equally swiftly, giving it just the right turn of phrasing that added point and pungence—or when, seizing on a "visit" suggestion, he would put on his hat and, demon reporter-like, go out to get the material for a piece on some landmark or other in our ever-beguiling city and come back and write it in time for our Thursday deadline. He may not have been so hot about four-alarm fires in Brooklyn, but he was just about unbeatable on such as these.

"Reality Twisted to the Right":
My Life and Hard Times

by Charles S. Holmes

The peak achievement of Thurber's early career is *My Life and Hard Times*. For many readers it is his one unquestioned masterpiece. Dwight MacDonald called it the best humor to come out of the entire post-World War I period.[1] Ernest Hemingway, in a letter to the publishers reprinted on the dust jacket, called Thurber's work as a whole "the best writing coming out of America." Of *My Life and Hard Times,* he said, tongue well implanted in cheek, "I find it far superior to the autobiography of Henry Adams. Even in the earliest days when Thurber was writing under the name of Alice B. Toklas we knew he had it in him if he could get it out." In spite of the heavy clowning, Hemingway's letter is a remarkable endorsement of a comparative unknown by one of the great modern stylists.

The book is the definitive image of Thurber's special comic world. Here the eccentric characters, chaotic situations, and the strange blend of the realistic and the fantastic which are the hallmarks of his work are present in their purest and most concentrated form. It mines one of his richest veins of subject matter—the days of his youth in Columbus—and out of these autobiographical materials he creates a mad comic world in which the normal order of things is constantly exploding into chaos and confusion. In Max Eastman's *The Enjoyment of Laughter* (1936), Thurber defined humor as "emotional chaos told about calmly and quietly in retrospect" (appropriating Wordsworth's famous theory of poetry to

" 'Reality Twisted to the Right': *My Life and Hard Times*" (editor's title). From Charles S. Holmes, "Columbus Remembered: *My Life and Hard Times*" in *The Clocks of Columbus* (New York: Atheneum Publishers, Inc., 1972). Copyright © 1972 by Charles S. Holmes. Reprinted by permission of the author, Atheneum Publishers, U.S.A., and Martin Secker & Warburg Ltd.

[1] Dwight MacDonald, "Laugh and Lie Down," *Partisan Review,* IV (December, 1937), 49.

justify a levity of which Wordsworth might not have approved),[2] and no better illustration of this theory than *My Life and Hard Times* could be imagined. The titles of the various chapters emphasize the theme of comic disorder—"The Night the Bed Fell," "The Day the Dam Broke," "The Night the Ghost Got In," "More Alarms at Night," and so on.

Disorder and confusion are anathema to the world at large, but for Thurber they are sources of value. They are at the heart of a set of closely related ideals which, until his very last years, he habitually champions in opposition to the dominant ideals of contemporary society. In a world committed to logic, organization, conformity, and efficiency, Thurber stands for fantasy, spontaneity, idiosyncrasy, and confusion. Hence Thurber's fondness for situations involving eccentric behavior, elaborate practical jokes, breakdowns of communication, and the disruption of bureaucratic machinery. Hence also his fondness for original and unconventional people like Grandfather, the Civil War veteran, who was never quite sure whether he was living in 1864 or 1910, and whose efforts to drive the electric automobile exhibit the family incompetence with machines and gadgets in its purest form; or Aunt Sarah Shoaf, who went to bed every night fearing that a burglar was going to get in and blow chloroform under her door with a tube, and so piled all her valuables outside, with a note reading, "This is all I have. Please take it and do not use your chloroform as this is all I have." The whole of *My Life and Hard Times* is a celebration of what might be called the Principle of Confusion, or the Fantasy-Principle. Nearly every episode shows the disruption of the orderly pattern of everyday life by the idiosyncratic, the irrational, the unpredictable.

"The Night the Bed Fell," for example, deals with chaos in the domestic circle. Father's unwonted decision to sleep in the attic one night, "to be away where he could think" and mother's certainty that the old bed up there would fall on Father and kill him set in motion a chain of events reminiscent of the scenes of comic anarchy in G. W. Harris's Sut Lovingood tales, or in Faulkner's "Spotted Horses." The trouble starts when the rather unstable army cot on which Thurber is sleeping tips over with a crash. . . . Cousin Briggs Beall, who lived in fear that some night he would stop breathing and always kept a glass of spirits of camphor at his bedside, starts awake with the terrifying certainty that he is suffocating

---

[2] Max Eastman, *The Enjoyment of Laughter* (New York: Simon & Schuster, 1936), p. 342.

and pours the camphor all over himself. Choking, he throws himself
at a window which is unfortunately closed. . . . Father, awakened
by Mother's banging on the attic door, thinks that the house is on
fire and calls out, " 'I'm coming.' " Mother, more than a little confused, cries out, " 'He's dying!' " . . . Father finally appears.
" 'What in the name of God is going on here?' " he asks. Things
finally get sorted out, and Mother, "who always looked on the bright
side of things," remarks to the boys, " 'I'm glad that your grandfather wasn't here.' "

"The Day the Dam Broke" tells of chaos in the community at
large. When someone shouts "The dam has broken!" during the
great flood of March, 1913, the quiet orderly life of Columbus explodes into panic and hysteria. Within minutes after the cry is
raised, two thousand people are rushing through the streets crying
"Go east! Go east!"—away from the river. Police and firemen and
army officers—guardians of order—join the fleeing mob: " 'Go
east!' " cried a little child in a piping voice, as she ran past a porch
on which drowsed a lieutenant-colonel of infantry. Used to quick
decisions, trained to immediate obedience, the officer bounded off
the porch and running at full tilt, soon passed the child, bawling
" 'Go east!' "

The fact that no one on the East Side was in any danger gives
Thurber's account of "the fine despair and the grotesque desperation" which seized the neighborhood a kind of mock-epic irony.
His manner as he tells the story of this day of community madness
is that of the historian—detached, objective, orderly—and much of
the comic value of his account lies in the contrast between this sober
historian's manner and the bizarre and fantastic events being described. He once remarked that if there was one thing identifiable
as a *New Yorker* style, it would be the habit of understatement,
"playing it down," [3] and the combination of dream-like unreality
and reportorial matter-of-factness in this description of how they
got Grandfather out of the house is a good example:

> We had to stun Grandfather with the ironing board. Impeded as
> we were by the inert form of the old gentleman—he was taller
> than six feet and weighed almost a hundred and seventy pounds
> —we were passed, in the first half-mile by practically everybody else
> in the city. Had grandfather not come to, at the corner of Parsons
> Avenue and Town Street, we would unquestionably have been
> overtaken and engulfed by the roaring waters—that is, if there
> had *been* any roaring waters.

[3] Interview with Plimpton and Steele, in *Writers at Work,* p. 88.

My Life and Hard Times is obviously a special kind of autobiography, existing somewhere between the world of fact and the
world of fantasy. Mother, Father, Grandfather, Thurber's two
brothers, some of the servants, the family dogs and local characters
like the Get-Ready Man are historically real. Thurber's bed did fall
down one night, there was a day of panic in Columbus during the
flood of 1913, and the boys did hear ghostly footsteps on the stairs.
The basic pattern of people and events is real enough, but woven
into this warp of truth is a cross-pattern of absurd and fanciful
details which transforms the actual into a strange world where confusion and eccentricity are the primary ways of life. Thurber pointed
to this mixture as a basic characteristic of his work as a whole when
he said to Robert van Gelder in an interview of 1940 that his writing
was based on truth, distorted for emphasis and amusement. "Reality
twisted to the right into humor rather than to the left into tragedy,"
he called it.[4]

Robert Thurber remembers that their father did on occasion
sleep in the attic and that one night the bed did collapse on him.
This domestic mishap was the germ of truth which set Thurber's
imagination to work. The wonderful concatenation of events in
Thurber's account of that wild night are his own embellishment of
what actually happened. They represent What Ought to Have Happened, if only the world were a little more artistically organized.
There was no such person as Cousin Briggs Beall, whose picturesque
neurosis adds so much to the nuttiness of the proceedings, and there
was no pandemonium in the hall when the bed fell. "My brother
leaned heavily on his imagination in this chapter," says Robert
Thurber.[5] On the other hand, some of the details of family eccentricity which strike the reader as most made up are simple truth.
Aunt Sarah Shoaf and her fear of burglars and chloroform are taken
from life, as is the conviction of Thurber's grandmother (in "The
Car We Had to Push") that electricity leaked out of empty light
sockets.

The great flood of March, 1913 was real enough. Dozens of Ohio
cities were inundated, and many people were drowned. The West
Side of Columbus was under thirty feet of water, bridges were swept
away, municipal services were paralyzed, and thousands of people
saw their homes destroyed. More than a hundred people lost their
lives. A headline in the Columbus *Dispatch* of March 26, 1913 reads,

4 *New York Times Book Review*, May 12, 1940, reprinted in van Gelder's *Writers and Writing*, p. 55.
5 Robert Thurber, letter to CSH, July 4, 1966.

SCENES OF DIRE/DESOLATION GREET/RESCUE PARTIES/ ON THE WEST SIDE/HUNDREDS ARE BROUGHT TO/ PLACES OF SAFETY BY DISPATCH/RELIEF EXPEDITION/. MANY ARE STILL IN PERIL/MANY CLING TO TREES/. The panic over the report that the dam had broken is also a matter of historical fact. Neil Martin, a Columbus newspaperman, recalled that memorable day in a story on Thurber in the Columbus *Citizen,* in 1952: "I do not believe any one can really, wholly appreciate Thurber who didn't participate in the Great Run on the day the Scioto River dam didn't break . . . on March 12, 1913," he wrote. "I was one of the several thousand who joined in the run and I have reason to think that none of us ever after was able to take himself too seriously." 6 The flood and the panic are historical facts, but almost all the details of Thurber's account—the lieutenant-colonel of infantry, Aunt Edith Taylor's remarkable long-distance run, and Grandfather's conviction that the city was under attack by Nathan Bedford Forrest's cavalry—are fanciful inventions designed to heighten the absurdity already implicit in the whole preposterous episode. . . .

Confusion, chaos, eccentricity—these are the qualities Thurber discovers and delights in as he looks back at the world of his boyhood, and in telling the story of those early days he consistently reshapes reality, stylizes and fictionalizes it, to bring it closer to the world of fantasy. Long before he put any of it down on paper, he was thinking about it, working it over in his memory and imagination, shaping it into anecdotes for the entertainment of his friends at parties. Thurber alludes to the dramatic origin of his stories in the opening paragraph of "The Night the Bed Fell": "It makes a better recitation (unless, as some friends of mine have said, one has heard it five or six times) than it does a piece of writing, for it is almost necessary to throw furniture around, shake doors, and bark like a dog, to lend the proper atmosphere. . . ." By the time he came to write it all down, fact and fantasy had become so perfectly assimilated to one another that there was no longer any noticeable difference between them.

The figure of Grandfather, whose airy disregard of the real world contributes so much to the zany atmosphere of the book as a whole, is perhaps the best example of the way in which Thurber's comic imagination transforms the facts of history in *My Life and Hard Times.* William M. Fisher, Thurber's real-life grandfather, is the

6 Columbus *Citizen* Magazine Section, June 22, 1952 (RTS).

subject of one of the portraits in *The Thurber Album*: in actuality he was a well-established Columbus business man and lived with his wife in a fine house on Bryden Road; he never saw military service, although he was a Civil War buff and a great reader of Grant's *Memoirs*; he had trouble learning to drive the car, and he had his little eccentricities, like walking to work every morning with a rose between his teeth; but he never got the past and the present mixed up, he never shot a policeman under the impression that he was a deserter from General Meade's army, and he never tried to enlist in World War I.

The fire-breathing old Civil War veteran of *My Life and Hard Times*, who prefers to live in the heroic past rather than the commonplace present, is almost entirely a fictional creation. As Thurber remakes him, he is the living embodiment of the superiority of the fantasy principle. Apparently infirm of mind and incapable of coping with the world of things as they are, Grandfather is in fact superior to it. He transcends it in his dream life, but he returns to it when he wants to. When the police invade the sanctuary of his attic bedroom looking for burglars on the memorable night the ghost got in, Grandfather is convinced that they are deserters from General Meade's army. Clad in his long flannel nightgown and nightcap, he confronts them, disarms one policeman and wings another. The rest beat a hasty retreat. Having triumphed over the real world in the skirmish of the night, he triumphs again at the breakfast table. While the members of the family wonder whether the old man remembers what happened, he glares at Thurber and brother Herman and asks, " 'What was the idee of all them cops tarryhootin' round the house last night?' "

Throughout *My Life and Hard Times* eccentricity of character is seen as a life-enhancing value. The mild insanities and picturesque obsessions of the people Thurber remembers from the days of his youth are not only diverting examples of the human comedy, they are also something important—they represent freedom, independence, the irrepressible stuff of life which refuses to be caught in formulas and conventions. Even the household pets showed the family strain of idiosyncrasy. Muggs, the burly, brooding Airedale who bit everybody, even members of the family, gets a whole chapter to himself. In nearly every way, Muggs belied the old saw that the dog is man's best friend. Because he would bite when anyone reached towards him, even with a plate of food, the family had to put his plate on top of an old kitchen table. Thurber's drawing of Muggs at dinner, hind feet on a bench, forefeet on the table, stumpy tail

erect, his great head turned back over his shoulder, a surly and suspicious expression on his face, is an unforgettable impression of
eccentricity and bad temper. Mrs. Thurber felt a special maternal
protectiveness towards Muggs. He was not strong, she used to say,
and she once consulted a faith healer in the hopes that Harmonious
Vibrations could be imparted to a dog. But Muggs went on biting
people until the day he died. Over his grave, Thurber placed a
board on which he had written with indelible pencil, "Cave
Canem."

The conflict between the unique individual and the world of in-
stitutionalized systems and regulations is the theme of "University
Days." Thurber's inability to see through a microscope in the botany
lab is a challenge to the basic assumptions of science and mass education:

> "We'll try it," the professor said to me grimly, "with every adjust-
> ment of the microscope known to man. As God is my witness, I'll
> arrange this glass so that you see cells through it or I'll give up
> teaching . . ." He cut off abruptly for he was beginning to quiver
> all over, like Lionel Barrymore, and he genuinely wished to hold
> on to his temper; his scenes with me had taken a great deal out of
> him.

Throughout his account of his college career, Thurber pictures himself in the role of confused misfit and sad sack. He had trouble in
economics, because it came right after botany, and he used to get the
two subjects mixed up; in the required gymnasium course he was
not allowed to wear his glasses, and so he bumped into "professors,
horizontal bars, agricultural students, and swinging iron rings"; he
flunked Military Drill so often that by his senior year he had
"drilled longer than anyone else in the Western Conference." Looking back, Thurber remembers not the heroes and achievers, but those
whose failures were somehow memorable. There was Bolenciecwz, the
mighty tackle on the football team, who also had trouble with economics, "for while he was not dumber than an ox, he was not any
smarter"; and there was the agricultural student, a would-be journalist, who, when told to get some zip into his style, came up with
this unforgettable lead: " 'Who has noticed the sores on the tops
of the horses in the animal husbandry building?' "

In such sketches as "University Days" and "Draft Board Nights"
Thurber's inability to cope is seen as a secret source of strength, an
oblique way of preserving his identity against the forces which would
rob him of it. Here, the Perfect Fool becomes a kind of hero. Most

often, however, it is the liabilities of the role of comic victim which
Thurber emphasizes, like the night the ghost got in, and he had to
explain to a couple of skeptical cops the presence of a zither in one
of the upstairs closets. Clad only in a pair of trousers, he tries to
make sense out of it: " 'It's an old zither our guinea pig used to
sleep on,' I said."

Thurber sharpens this self-portrait in the "Preface to a Life" and
"A Note at the End" which frame his account of his early Columbus years. The "Preface" invites the reader to see the book as a
mock-autobiography, a parody of the great tradition represented by
Benvenuto Cellini, who said that a man should have accomplished
something of excellence before writing his life, and Ford Madox
Ford, who said that the sole reason for writing one's memoirs was to
paint a picture of one's time. This element of parody was what ap-
pealed to Hemingway, and when he jokingly compared Thurber's
book to *The Education of Henry Adams,* he was doubtless thinking
of the irony with which both autobiographers viewed themselves
and their achievements. Thurber points out that his only notable
accomplishment is his skill in "hitting empty ginger ale bottles with
small rocks at a distance of thirty paces," and that the time pictured
in the work of a writer of short humorous pieces would not be
"Walter Lippmann's time or Stuart Chase's time or Professor Ein-
stein's time," but a rather small and personal one, "circumscribed
by the short boundaries of his pain and embarrassment, in which
what happens to his digestion, the rear axle of his car, and the confused flow of his relationships with six or eight persons . . . is of
greater importance than what goes on in the nation or the universe."

He makes the same point—more indirectly—in the title of his
book: the phrase "Hard Times" would remind all readers that the
book was written in the middle of a great economic depression and
had absolutely nothing to say about it. The historian, the scientist,
and the social critic properly address themselves to the great issues
of the day, but the humorist should confine himself to the common
experience of the private individual, particularly to the trivia in
which every man's life is hopelessly entangled. Throughout the
1930's he steadfastly resisted the pressure on writers to make their
work socially significant. In later years he was to modify his view
and to see humor as a public force, a weapon for social good, rather
than as subjective experience, but at this stage of his career, he
obviously felt that the state of society and the crises of history were
not the best subjects for the humorist. . . .

The little autobiographical essays which frame *My Life and Hard Times* not only define the Thurber protagonist—a figure created out of himself, but with the neurotic and daydreamy aspects of his nature played up and the tough-mindedness and the professional expertise left out—but they also advance a psychological theory of humor to which he subscribed throughout his life. For Thurber, the twin sources of humor were always the misadventures of everyday life and the neuroses of the middle-class American male. "I think humor is the best that lies closest to the familiar, to that part of the familiar which is humiliating, distressing, even tragic," he said in his statement to Max Eastman. The emphasis in the "Preface" and the "Note" is on the distress and the humiliation. Humor is not "a joyous form of self-expression," he says, "but the manifestation of a twitchiness at once cosmic and mundane." The humorist writes not out of an overflow of genial spirits, but out of anxiety and fear: "the little wheels of his invention are set in motion by the damp hand of melancholy." The tone here is light and self-mocking, but the statement reveals an important truth about Thurber—that the dark strain in his nature was the primary force in his imaginative life. He made the same point, without the fictional mask, on a BBC program many years later. Humor was not a sign of balance, he said, but of counter-balance. It is a kind of therapy, a way of coping with one's inner terrors—and by implication, with those of the audience as well. "I don't know any American humorist, including myself, who hasn't been in some kind of pretty serious mental emotional pathological psychopathic state," he said.[7]

Curiously, for all the Freudianism of his theory, Thurber has nothing to say, early or late, about humor as aggression. Yet few humorists have expressed our resentments and hostilities more brilliantly and more consistently than Thurber. For the author of "The Indian Sign," "A Couple of Hamburgers," "The Cane in the Corridor," "Am Not I Your Rosalind?," "The Secret Life of Walter Mitty," and "The Unicorn in the Garden" to be silent about humor as a form of psychological warfare is a strange and suggestive omission.

In the postwar era, when he became more and more concerned over what was happening to American life, Thurber had less to say about humor as the release of private anxiety and more to say about its broad moral and social function. He argued for humor as a nec-

[7] "Frankly Speaking," BBC Home Service Program, December 24, 1958.

essary weapon against the fanaticism of the McCarthy era. In a public speech, in 1953, he quoted E. B. White's remark that "humorous writing, like poetical writing, has an extra content. It plays, like an active child, close to the big hot fire which is Truth." [8] As his view of life became increasingly conservative, so did his theory of comedy. He disapproved of the "sick" humor which began to dominate the scene, and spoke of comedy more often in Meredithian than Freudian terms. In an age of vulgarized tastes and disintegrating standards, he looked to the comic spirit as "the saving grace," one of the few remaining forces of rationality and civility in a dark time.

[8] *Thurber on Humor,* the Martha Kinney Cooper Ohioana Library Association (Columbus, Ohio, 1953).

James Thurber's Style

by Michael Burnett

James Thurber had two basic and in some ways contradictory attitudes toward his profession, and thus held—usually in ironic tension—two attitudes toward language; hence, his style exhibits two basic tendencies, the collision of which forms the source for much of his humor. One tends to think of Thurber—a man who, after all, made his living writing for the very style-conscious *New Yorker*—as an adroit and inventive prose stylist, one who, through his verbal pyrotechnics, wrought humor out of the commonplace. Yet, in fact, Thurber's basic style is remarkably neutral, exhibiting a marked avoidance of verbal acrobatics. Thurber always regarded himself as a journalist, and much of his prose is written in the clear, flat, economical style of the reporter; it is a style which does its best not to call attention to itself through any deviations from the norm. Thurber was intensely concerned with the purity of the language, and he wrote many pieces decrying its abuse. Language, to Thurber, as Charles S. Holmes, in an essay on the humorist states, is "a necessary principle of order, and an instrument of precision and beauty," [1] a besieged force for clarity in an increasingly confusing world. Extremely traditionalist in his conception of style, he viewed the tampering with language on the part of advertising, politics, and various other specialized fields, with a growing alarm which amounted, in his later years, almost to an obsession.

Yet Thurber, and here we see the other side of his professional and hence stylistic coin, was an inveterate dabbler with language, "fascinated," as Holmes says, "by its capacity to create an Alice-in-Wonderland world where ordinary rational communication is transcended." [2] He was a connoisseur of chaos. To the journalist, then,

"James Thurber's Style," by Michael Burnett, Fairhaven College, Bellingham, Wash. © 1973 by Michael Burnett. Used by permission of the author. This article appears for the first time in this volume.

1 Charles S. Holmes, "James Thurber and the Art of Fantasy," *The Yale Review,* LV (October, 1965), 23.

2 Holmes, p. 23.

Thurber improbably grafted the fantasist; and out of the collision of the two (out of the collision of two styles and, finally, of two world views) issued his humor.

One who would define and analyze Thurber's style is faced, then, with a problem. In Thurber's early work, the journalist prevails, and the style is relatively neutral. In his later work, however, reflecting a more bitter attitude toward a growingly chaotic world, Thurber's prose is packed with puns, scrambled literary allusions, anagrams and other forms of wordplay, and sequences of words linked phonemically in a hectic conjunction in which meaning, ordered meaning, is lost; and characters, tricked by what was once an "instrument of precision," fall into the confusion of fantasy. Further, Thurber was a great parodist; to analyze the style of, say, "The Secret Life of Walter Mitty," "The White Rabbit Caper," or *The Thirteen Clocks* would be to track down, not Thurber, but Thurber as writer of the adventure tale, the murder mystery, and the fairy tale. One must finally, rather artificially, isolate a "base style," a style from which, for humorous or satiric purposes, Thurber will occasionally deviate. I have decided, then, to limit my discussion to *My Life and Hard Times*,[3] a volume which, I believe, best represents the quintessential Thurber, the mimic speaking in his own voice, the journalist whose taste for fantasy is under tight rational control.

This base style is not linguistically complex or idiosyncratically inventive. In the whole book there is not one pun. Indeed there are only two instances of wordplay, and both are mistakes characters make, reported in dialogue, and are thus not really aspects of *Thurber's* basic style at all. The first is the malapropism "The lady seems historical" (63), which capitalizes on the confusion of phonemes /ɔ/ and /ɛ/. The other is a bit of dialogue between an exasperated economics teacher and a big but stupid tackle, from whom the teacher is trying to elicit the word "train":

> "How did you come to college this year, Mr. Bolenciecwicz? . . ."
> "M'father sent me," said the football player.
> "What on?" asked Bassum.
> "I git an 'lowance," said the tackle . . . (119).

The tackle, of course, is mixing up the preposition with its usage in the idiom "on an allowance."

Thurber does invent words, but he uses them with surprising

3 James Thurber, *My Life and Hard Times* (New York, 1933). All references to page numbers are enclosed in parentheses.

infrequency. The following list exhausts those I found in the book:

1. Tires booped and whooshed, the fenders queeled and graked, the steering-wheel rose up like a spectre (26)
2. Ugf, ahfg (11) [phonetic representation of choking sounds]
3. Gugh (120)
4. Awp (55) [a fear-sound]
5. whammed it through a pane of glass (57)
6. she came flubbering up the cellar stairs (90)
7. we had begun to climb, clickety-clockety (142)

Only (1) and (6) seem to me to be newly created words, (2), (3), and (4) being merely transcriptions of sounds, (5) being a verb I've often encountered, and (7) being a modification of "clickety-clack," a common onomatopoetic phrase. Thus Thurber is little out of the ordinary in either morphemic or phonemic usage.

Nor is he especially striking in his syntax. He makes virtually no use of unusual word order, with the possible exception of an occasional initial placing of object: "My memories of what my family and I went through during the 1913 flood in Ohio I would gladly forget" (34), a usage by no means peculiar to Thurber. Clausal structure, and placement and frequency of subordinate clauses, seem in no way unusual. Although he does, occasionally, employ repetition for humorous effect, I counted only eleven significant instances of repetition. In almost all such cases, a word or phrase is repeated with no change in its shape, and is repeated in conscious avoidance of possible substitutions. In each case, the phrase is repeated in its entirety, thus giving an effect of "flatness," and often calling attention to the banality or idiomatic nature of the phrase:

1. "This is all I have. Please take it and do not use your chloroform, as this is all I have." (4)
2. "until it blows over." . . . after the war had blown over (29)
3. to tie the dog up, but mother said that it mortified him to be tied up and that he wouldn't eat when he was tied up (104)
4. we suddenly had mice . . . Nobody ever had mice like the mice we had that month. (94)
5. wouldn't go unless you pushed it for quite a way and suddenly let your clutch out. . . . it wouldn't go unless you pushed it and let your clutch out (16)

Thurber is scrupulous in following grammatical norms; only twice did I encounter a mixing of form-classes: "tall, hawk-nosed, round-oathed" (33), in which a noun-phrase is used as an adjective, and "watched with cold unconcern the going to pieces of the capital city" (47), in which an idiomatic verb-phrase is used as a noun. Very infrequently, and always with parodic intention, Thurber will indulge in substandard grammar:

1. He didn't act sorry. . . . he acted poisoned (95)
2. another a whole lot like him (121)
3. on account of having to hunt (122)

There is no definite indication that Thurber uses any particular form-class more than is normal. I have a suspicion that he tends to underuse adjectives (his descriptions tend to be generic and abstract, rather than richly particularized), and that he leans rather heavily on verbs of action, a usage I will discuss below, but only an exhaustive word count would test that suspicion.

I have, I believe, glanced at every aspect of style except diction; and it is in his diction that Thurber's humor lies. The base style, which I have called "journalistic," involves the rather colorless features—or rather *lack* of features, lack of morphemic, phonemic, syntactic, or grammatical experimentation—described above, and a rather stilted, archaic vocabulary, heavy in Latinisms, which reflects Thurber's nostalgia for past, more ordered, patterns of life and forms of expression:

1. under the deluge of pungent spirits (11)
2. Impeded as we were by the inert form of the old gentleman (39)
3. It is the way in which I and the other members of my family invariably allude to the occasion. (67)
4. I began to feel the imperative necessity of human contact. (73)
5. a nebulous milky substance—a phenomenon of maladjustment (111)
6. the familiar lacteal opacity (112)
7. her first vehicular triumph (131)

He will often use phrases, to introduce or further his narrative, drawn from the repertoire of the nineteenth-century storyteller, and reminiscent of, say, Henry James, who was Thurber's favorite author:

1. It was at this juncture (11)
2. She could only suppose (25)

3. On the night in question, however (68)
4. It was some six months after this that father went through a similar experience with me. (72)
5. But I am straying from the remarkable incidents that took place during the night (7)

In contrast, but in conjunction with this ordered, formal, impersonal, slightly archaic diction, is a vast amount of idiom, often expressive of violent action and chaotic and idiosyncratic states of mind, but almost invariably, also, nostalgic, in that these usages belong mainly to the rural, familial past of Thurber's childhood:

1. who had his crotchets (3)
2. newfangled (25)
3. safe as kittens under a cookstove (40)
4. raised such a hullabaloo (52)
5. pretty well nettled (71)
6. brown as a berry (111)
7. he let go with his swatter (125)

In further humorous juxtaposition with the neutral base style are a great number of verbs of strenuous action, seemingly expressive of contests or battles:

1. *drubbed* it unmercifully (26)
2. we slowly began to *gain on* those ahead of us (43)
3. a fat, waddling man . . . *intercepted* the colonel (44)
4. *pushing* and *shoving* and *clawing, knocking* women and children down, emerging . . . torn and *sprawling* (46)
5. *creeping up on* the old chemistry building (123)

In contrast both with the base style and with the events described (which, I should mention, are usually of the most ordinary, simple nature), Thurber uses a whole range of words and phrases found normally in contexts of danger and intrigue; this is the diction of the mystery novel or the romance:

1. Her greatest dread (25)
2. dangerous leakage (26) ["Dangerous" is an extremely common word in Thurber.].
3. came to a horrible end (26)
4. the horrible suspicion (25)
5. frightful and perilous afternoon (34)
6. it was a common subterfuge (138)

In an interesting use of collocation, Thurber, in describing people and their actions, will often use terms applicable mainly to animals:

1. Another man, a portly gentleman of affairs, broke into a trot. (42)
2. he jogged on east again (48)
3. he said, in the low, hopeless tone of a despondent beagle (55)
4. My brother Herman finally felled her. (86)

Finally, Thurber uses a great many proper names, with an effect similar to that produced by his use of idiom. The presence of the names of streets in Columbus, Ohio; of actors or movie stars, of various makes of automobiles, and of brands of merchandise, is ludicrous in its specificity. All the apparatus of an impersonal, crisp journalistic style, fraught with diction expressive of events and people of significance, is brought to bear upon simple, ordinary men and the events of daily existence. The effect is that of the mock-heroic: inflated diction is satirized, the people and events described are satirized, and, finally, in spite of the satire involved, those people and events take on a kind of heroic, if nostalgic, dignity commensurate with the language in which they are treated.

A glance at a passage will illustrate the functioning of Thurber's style. This is the beginning passage from the story "The Day the Dam Broke," its sentences, for ease of reference, separated and numbered:

1. My memories of what my family and I went through during the 1913 flood in Ohio I would gladly forget.
2. And yet neither the hardships we endured nor the turmoil and confusion we experienced can alter my feeling toward my native state and city.
3. I am having a fine time now and wish Columbus were here, but if anyone ever wished a city was in hell it was during that frightful and perilous afternoon in 1913 when the dam broke or, to be more exact, when everybody in town *thought* that the dam broke.
4. We were both ennobled and demoralized by the experience.
5. Grandfather especially rose to magnificent heights which can never lose their splendor for me, even though his reactions to the flood were based upon a profound misconception; namely, that Nathan Bedford Forrest's cavalry was the menace we were called upon to face.

6. The only possible means of escape for us was to flee the house, a step which grandfather sternly forbade, brandishing his old army sabre in his hand.

7. "Let the sons —— come!" he roared.

8. Meanwhile hundreds of people were streaming by our house in wild panic, screaming "Go east! Go east!"

9. We had to stun grandfather with the ironing board.

10. Impeded as we were by the inert form of the old gentleman —he was taller than six feet and weighed almost a hundred and seventy pounds—we were passed, in the first half-mile, by practically everybody else in the city.

11. Had grandfather not come to, at the corner of Parsons Avenue and Town Street, we would unquestionably have been over-taken and engulfed by the roaring waters—that is, if there had *been* any roaring waters.

Notice, first of all, that the three longest sentences in the passage, (3), (5), and (11), all work in the same way. An initial, specific, and, in two cases, colloquial reference [in (5) this is only the proper name, "grandfather"] is followed by a long, rhetorical locution, which is ironically belied by the flat facts of the case. This very typical structure operates throughout the passage. The placement of object before subject in sentence (1) has already been mentioned; by locating "forget" at the end of the sentence Thurber puts it in humorous balance with the initial "My memories." The initial con-junction in sentence (2) is not strikingly characteristic of Thurber. The diction of sentence (2) is appropriate to the reporting of actual flood conditions, rather than to illusory—or fantasy—ones. The balance of phrases introduced by "neither . . . nor" is character-istic; Thurber's prose becomes more ordered and symmetrical the more chaotic the scene he describes. Sentence (3) opens with a varia-tion on the colloquial idiomatic phrase "having a fine time; wish you were here," and continues with a variation on another idio-matic phrase "go to hell," in humorous parallel and contrast. Both colloquialisms are in contrast with the formal diction of both sen-tence (2) and of the phrase "during that frightful and perilous after-noon in 1913," in sentence (3). The admission at the end of sentence (3)—that the danger was illusory—makes the diction of sentence (4) mock-heroic, an effect heightened by the latter sentence's relative shortness. Sentence (5) opens with "Grandfather," used as a proper noun; this humorously locates the recipient of the elaborate and inflated locution "rose to magnificent heights which can never lose their splendor for me" in a specific and limited individual. Similarly, the noun-phrase "Nathan Bedford Forrest's cavalry," with its specific proper name, stands paled by the generalized, apocalyptic diction of "the menace we were called upon to face," the whole qualified, of course, by the fact that all this heroic diction is brought to bear upon "a profound misconception." Energetic verbs ("flee," "forbade," "brandishing," "roared," "streaming," "screaming," "stun") give a tone of chaos which contrasts with the sedate archaic diction of "Impeded as we were by the inert form of the old gentleman." The extremely funny incongruity of sentence (9) is due, insofar as that humor has a stylistic source, to what can only be termed "understatement." A violent and unusual act is mentioned —but not described—in totally neutral style, in one of the shortest sentences in the passage. The word "stun" seems improper in collocation with "grandfather," being normally applied, when used as a transitive verb, mainly to beasts. And an ironing board is hardly of the class of objects usually considered as weapons! The colloquial phrasal verb "come to," in sentence (11), and the proper names of streets—names ostensibly provided in the interest of journalistic accuracy, an accuracy mitigated by the fact that they are so localized as to be unfamiliar to the reader—clash with the diction of the phrase "would unquestionably have been overtaken and engulfed by the roaring waters." The whole superstructure of catastrophe somberly reported by the above phrase collapses—and its unreality is emphasized by the unchanged repetition of "roaring waters"—when we realize that all has been a fantasy on the part of the townspeople.

Professor Holmes says that "The essential quality of Thurber's imagination is the tension between a strong sense of fact (throughout his life he considered himself primarily a journalist) and a strong bias toward fantasy." [4] Thurber's style, as we have seen, reflects this tension, and effects its resolution into humor.

4 Holmes, p. 33.

Thurber through British Eyes

by David Garnett

"The learned Doctor James Thurber," as his publishers call him, is at present, I think, the most original and humorous writer living, so it is interesting to see what will become of him. Great humorists start as solitary men, their laughter is first thought to be a sign of insanity; presently everyone begins to see their jokes, or laughs with them, and they become pneumatic cushions for humanity. How will Thurber support the massive weight with which we threaten him? For many years Thurber was a newspaper reporter who expressed his private feelings by quick scribbles. His friends saw their quality and showed them to editors who stared and finally printed them, though convinced the man who drew them must be crazy. In spite of such misgivings the drawings caught on; Thurber amused and became known to millions—and at the same time he began to write. His first book, *Is Sex Necessary?*, was a piece of collaboration aimed at the popular psychologists and psychoanalysts. It is very funny, on the lines of the ordinary funny book. *My Life and Hard Times* was, as its title indicates, an autobiographical sketch of early years in Columbus, Ohio, and is one of the funniest and most lovable books I know; the humour is intensely original and individual; every man, woman and dog in it has an overpowering personality. *The Middle-Aged Man on the Flying Trapeze* is a collection of stories of varying quality. Some of them have an extremely penetrating savage humour of the kind which scares the ordinary person. Women are roughly handled, and, in "A Box to Hide In," Thurber shows what he feels of the attractions of the world. That story is, incidentally, one of the most alarming things in literature. But since we all long for a chance to laugh, the crowd has been growing and Thurber has now a very large audience. He himself is feeling more comfortable, and he naturally has become

less savage and more serious. Thus in *Let Your Mind Alone . . .*
he returns to the subject of *Is Sex Necessary?* with an onslaught
on the quack psychologists and system-mongers who sell their quick
roads to success, to character building, to "mental-efficiency" and
"masterful adjustment," to the American and British public. Thus,
Let Your Mind Alone is an attack on a lot of half-baked ideas. For
example, in *Sex Ex Machina* he attacks the popularisers of Freud
who explain the pedestrian's wavering and hesitation in front of
traffic by his sexual mal-adjustment, since "the automobile serves
as a sex-symbol because of the mechanical principle involved." (The
quotation is genuine and not a parody.) Thurber suggests man may
recognise the menace of the machine as such.

> You can see the result, entirely unsuperinduced by sex in the
> strained faces and muttering lips of the people who pass you on the
> streets of great, highly mechanized cities. There goes a man who
> picked up one of those trick match-boxes that whirr in your hands,
> there goes a woman who tried to change a fuse without turning
> off the current and yonder toddles an ancient who cranked an old
> Reo with the spark advanced. Every person carries in his con-
> sciousness the old scar, or the fresh wound, of some harrowing
> misadventure with a contraption of some sort.

Near by is a picture of a *Happily mated rabbit terrified of motor
car,* which has all the floppy action of Mr. Thurber's bloodhounds.
He points out that rabbits are as ignorant of sex symbolism as most
women are of "the mechanical principle involved" in motor cars.
It is very amusing, very sensible, but much too good-tempered.

In other chapters Thurber makes fun of the professors who tell
one how "to streamline one's mind," how "to worry successfully,"
how to impress one's superiors in business by writing crisp uncalled-
for memoranda, and he breaks off suddenly to tell us how his Aunt
Kate ran a large dairy successfully.

> Shouldering her way past a number of dairy workers, farm
> hands, and members of her family, she grasped the cream separator
> and began monkeying with it. In a short time she had reduced it
> to even more pieces than it had been in when she took hold of it.
> She couldn't fix it. She was just making things worse. At length
> she turned on the onlookers and bawled: "Why doesn't someone
> take this goddam thing away from me?"

Thurber has inherited and expanded his Aunt Kate's philosophy
—which, as he points out, won her more love and respect than if

she had behaved on the lines of the success booklets. But, though perhaps he could not tackle a separator, he scores vindictively over Dr. Sadie Shellow, sometime psychologist to the Milwaukee Railway, tripping her up in her own intelligence test

> which I can only call a paradise of errors. I find in Dr. Shellow's presentation of the problem and her solution of it, Transference, Wishful Thinking, Unconscious Sublimation, Psychological Dissociation, Gordian Knot-cutting, Cursory Enumeration, Abandonment of Specific Gravity. . . .

Most of us, in Thurber's phrase, will "string along with him" against the streamlined mind and efficiency experts. But don't let's be too rumbustious or we may be thinking that all psychologists are comic. It is fatally easy for the humorist to turn from attacking half-baked ideas to attacking ideas as such—and if he does he will be sure to have the vast majority of humanity (who were laughing at him a few years ago because they thought him crazy) "stringing along with him." I utter this solemn word of warning thinking of the terrible fate of Mark Twain, whose genius was deflected into ridiculing history, and all forms of art everywhere. He won the gratitude of millions of his fellow-countrymen and the position of a prophet, by reassuring them that they missed nothing by ignoring every sort of aesthetic and intellectual culture. It would be far better to be thought a mad artist and string along with a lobster like Gérard de Nerval (who also was a very great writer), than to be the lobster which the American nation takes on a string like Twain. The American nation can pull harder than the humorist. Thurber would hate such a position, yet in the following passage Mark Twain might be speaking from his grave.

> I have arrived at what I call Thurber's Law, which is that scientists don't really know anything about anything. . . . Scientists just think light is going that fast because they are afraid of it. . . . I have always suspected that light just plodded along, and now I am sure of it.

Such dismal fears, I must say, are not substantiated by a prophecy of the future called "After the Steppe Cat, What?" in which Thurber's imagination runs away with him as he foretells the decay of human civilisation and describes the cloud of mantises which fell on the New York skyscrapers, peering in at the office windows to spy out the chinks in man's armour. He enumerates the weevil, the wombat, the rabbit, the aardvark, the bandicoot, the Scotch terrier, the cockroach, the codling moth and the Colorado beetle, to name just a few of the thousands of insects and animals who will all come to town when the Great Invasion begins.

For all living things will then co-operate to wrest power from man, who has been keeping a fearful eye on his fellowman, to the exclusion of the Steppe cat and the Steppe cat's million allies.

Look through your field glasses at the nearest Steppe land—close to the ground. There—see that greyish white blurr with the blackish transverse bars.

There is a wild poetry about the Steppe cat which recalls not Mark Twain, but Edward Lear. I really enjoy Thurber most (and feel he is on safest ground) when he doesn't deal with ideas or institutions, but with personal experiences, and when he's not trying to be funny at all. Three such chapters in this book have for me an inexplicable charm. "The Wood Duck" is simply a piece of realism —describing a wild duck which left the woods, preferring to live near a roadside apple-stand on a concrete highway, black in the centre with the dropped oil of a million cars. It is a perfect short dramatic story. "Memories of D. H. Lawrence" and "Doc Marlowe" and "The Wood Duck" make me believe that Thurber will have sufficient strength of character and is enough of an artist to refuse to be forcibly made a Twain of, and that he will develop along his own lines as a first-rate writer and not as a funny man or a prophet.

James Thurber: the Primitive, the Innocent, and the Individual

by Robert H. Elias

The angel that writes names in a book of gold must long ago have put McNulty down as one who delighted in his fellow man. His delight in human beings was warm and deep and, though he deserved to be called a social critic, he was concerned mainly with men, not Man, with persons, not People.

James Thurber, "My Friend McNulty"
(*The World of John McNulty*, 1957)

For more than a generation James Thurber has been writing stories, an impressive number of them as well shaped as the most finely wrought pieces of Henry James, James Joyce and Ernest Hemingway, as sensitively worded as the most discriminatingly written prose of H. L. Mencken, Westbrook Pegler and J. D. Salinger, and as penetrating—especially during what we can call his "major phase"—as the most pointed insights of those two large poets of our century, E. A. Robinson and Robert Frost. Yet, slightly older than Hemingway and Faulkner, he has been the subject of no full-length studies, nor has he been prominently mentioned, as he long ago should have been, for the Nobel Prize. In fact, it is only within the past four years that he has been treated to any adequately extended critical consideration at all. For the most part, when he has not been dismissed as simply a cartoonist, he has been condemned by a conglomeration of whimsical reviews, human interest features full of newsworthy legends and pictures, and that extinguisher of merit, the label, to the minor category of humorist

—a kind of latter-day Mark Twain saved from the lamented excesses by *New Yorker* sophistication. The truth, however, is that among our living writers he is virtually our only creator of serious comedy and one of the few humanists who can make an affirmation without either a chip or a Christ symbol on his shoulder. Indeed, in Thurber's prose the individual is best off when freed of all the paraphernalia of systems, whether mechanical, social, literary or just plain transcendental.

Now none of this is to imply that Thurber is not a humorist at all. It is a dull mind that can see nothing funny in the antics of *My Life and Hard Times,* or the satire of *Let Your Mind Alone,* or the practical jokes of Thurber's mother and of Birdey Doggett, or the denouement of "The Catbird Seat." But it is to suggest that if anyone thinks *My Life and Hard Times* is most representative of Thurber's accomplishment, he has overlooked the more vital and rewarding Thurber, embodied, to be sure, with humor but often with grim urgency, in the work he has produced during the past nineteen years, ranging from "The Secret Life of Walter Mitty" (1939) to his newest story, *The Wonderful O* (1957).

What needs most to be emphasized today to show how much Thurber deserves serious attention is that the central concern of Thurber's best stories—and these may be rooted in either his personal experience or his imagination—is nothing less than the predicament of the individual in our gadget-cluttered, career-woman-dominated, theory-burdened time. Thurber's protagonists, usually but not always men, may be perplexed by cars that will not start, driven to divorce by women who will not let them read their paper, or reduced to the data of equations by social and psychological engineers who explain away volition; but consistently they are engaged in self-preservation—struggling to keep inviolate the realms of chance, individuality, reflection and purpose, which give the will substance to work with and freedom occasion for exercise. The self, as Thurber shows, is in danger of extinction when persons are driven inward until society becomes impossible, or forced outward until there is no residue to socialize. The most interesting aspect of Thurber's artistic development is in terms of his search for a place where the individual can finally reside—or preside.

Since almost the beginning of his career as a story writer Thurber has insisted that the menace to the individual lurks in the world of man-made systems, whether mechanical or mental, and that the promise waits in the uncircumscribed realms of instinct and the imagination. In *Is Sex Necessary?*, written with E. B. White in 1929, Thurber engages in an amusing satire on the "deep and lugubrious books on sex and marriage" produced in the twenties, when "the human animal seemed [so] absorbed in self-analysis" that he transformed sex from physical expression into something mental. The notable first chapter, "The Nature of the American Male, a Study of Pedestalism," written by Thurber, caricatures the formula-ridden historians of society and sex and, basing its argument largely on the case of the frustrated real estate man, George Smith, exposes the pretentious futility of psychoanalysts. Smith, tortured for three years by the unresponsiveness of a maiden whose love he craves, in vain seeks fulfillment by trying to solve pigs-in-clover puzzles. His failure leads to a "Magnification of Object" that his doctor's "analytic reasoning" and prescription of "cold applications" cannot reduce. He readily rids himself of all his problems, however, when, his door closed to his doctor, he by sheer chance breaks the glass of one of the boxes and pushes the little balls into their corners with his finger. This may be ridicule, but it is at the same time not ridiculous criticism. Where, according to Thurber, the Chinese see love as biology and the French see it as biology with humor, Americans regard it as two-thirds psyche and, confusing the psychical with the physical, conclude by also confusing appetite with worship that is as bad for sex as it is for soul. Exegetes enter where men fear to tread, and analysis becomes action's only name.

The question posed in Thurber's stories, however, is usually less whether action is valid than what it is opposed to or by. In *Is Sex Necessary?* it is opposed to analysis by rigid rule and to a denial of natural inclinations. George Smith is a free man once he locks his analyst out and lets happen what will. In the stories that soon followed concerning Mr. and Mrs. Monroe (in *The Owl in the Attic*, 1931) action is identified with a mastery of the practical world, with a kind of conventional social adjustment, and is opposed to dreams, romance, the ideals of heroic fulfillment. Mr. Monroe is no more a hero to us than he is to his wife (or in reality to himself—"a tall thin man looks like an ass in socks and garters," he thinks, standing before his mirror); yet our sympathies are as much with him as they are with George Smith, for he is an individual who cannot conform, who resists the consuming effects of actuality. John Monroe "likes to brood and reflect and occasionally to catch glimpses of himself in store windows . . . brooding and reflecting." He can never take a shower successfully because "he always gets the water to running too cold or too hot." He cannot match his wife's poise in smuggling a dozen bottles of Benedictine through the customs.

He cannot tell packers and movers which household objects go into storage and which to the country place. As Thurber informs us, in a rare comment:

> He had a certain charm, yes; but not character. He evaded diffi-cult situations; he had no talent for firm resolution; he immolated badly; and he wasn't even very good at renunciation, except when he was tired or a little sick. Not, you will see, the man to move household goods into storage when his wife is away.

Indeed, he cannot kill a bat that is on the wing outside the bed-room, sleep in the house alone when escaped convicts are sure to be roaming the woods outside, or carry out an adulterous affair whose challenge plunges him simply into reveries, into a three-minute sleepy go at *The Golden Bowl* as preparation for a mature communion, and finally into pajamas and his own bed, where he can at least master sleep.

We sympathize, I think, because for all his ineffectualness he represents the alternative to cocksureness, to complacency or satis-faction with given formulations. If great deeds are to be done, they will not be done by customs officials or moving men. They may be done by wives, but not in the realm that the brooders and reflectors inhabit—the realm of artists and other dreamers. Mr. Monroe, to be sure, will produce no work of art, and Thurber's treatment of him is, as the fashionable word is, ambivalent. Nevertheless, Mr. Monroe is our man; he is, as it were, one of us.

What both Smith and Monroe have in common, then, is a kind of eccentricity—they are a little off social center; their conduct deviates from the norm, whether that norm be the one set by psy-choanalysts for defining the abnormal or whether it be the one assumed by the packers who preserve the china in sawdust. And this deviation is good; it wins us. The parodies in *The Owl in the Attic* of the *New York Evening Post*'s Pet Department and of Fowler's *Dictionary of Modern English Usage* are but further con-firmation of the satisfaction that comes in challenging formulas that pretentiously fail to account for human peculiarities.

If anyone doubts the character of Thurber's affirmation, *My Life and Hard Times* (1933) should dissipate the doubt at once. Al-though Thurber writes mainly about the decade preceding the First World War, one is scarcely aware that the past may have been sought by the writer as escape. The positive value of being at odds with the facts of a commonplace world is what dominates the book. In the role of a narrator who has reminded some readers of a comic

Prufrock, Thurber relates that his cousin Briggs Beall believed he was likely to cease breathing when he was asleep, that Aunt Sarah Shoaf never went to bed without a fear that a burglar was going to break into the house and blow chloroform under her door through a tube, that his own brother sometimes sang "Marching Through Georgia" and "Onward, Christian Soldiers" in his sleep, and that his father had at least once gone to sleep in the attic in order to think (once, that is, when Grandfather, still fighting the Civil War, was on an expedition to check up on the Army of the Potomac). Thurber tells of numerous incidents in which there is a farcical non-meeting of minds. The family gets the notion that Father is being crushed in his attic bed, or that ghosts have broken in; thousands in Columbus during the 1913 floods mistakenly infer that the dam has given way and flee eastward. When people live in their special and peculiar spheres, uproarious misunderstandings compose the daily round; and we enjoy them, just as we enjoy the crotchets of Thurber's relatives. After all, to believe as did his grandmother that electricity was dripping invisibly all over the house, or as did his mother that it was dangerous to drive a car without gasoline because it fried the valves or something, is a sign of blameless, innocent faith—not in the world but at least in the accuracy of one's own unduplicated perceptions. To these persons it is the machines that make no good sense and that pose the needless dangers. In those days, to be alive must have been very heaven indeed.

But this celebration of the sources of hullabaloo is necessarily qualified as Thurber comes to confront the predicament of the ordinary man in his own time. "In the pathways between office and home and home and the houses of settled people," Thurber writes, "there are, always ready to snap at you, the little perils of routine living, but there is no escape in the unplanned tangent, the sudden turn." The case of George Smith serves better to refute someone else's generalization than to objectify an actual society, and an older generation's oddities, however delightful, cannot adequately enable a responsible person to come to terms with himself in the present. In the appropriately titled *The Middle-Aged Man on the Flying Trapeze* (1935) and in *Let Your Mind Alone* (1937) there are still, one hastens to acknowledge, individuals who in various funny ways cannot be pigeonholed—individuals who manufacture their own facts to account for the world. Aunt Ida, who thinks the *Titanic*'s iceberg was a monstrous fiction to mask corporate corruption and expects a comet to do the world in any day; Jad Peters, who figures out lucky escapes he could have had from every disaster that has happened in Sugar Grove and comes to tell how he did have them; Thurber himself as distraught narrator, harassed by the hazards of wearing an overcoat that helpful doormen and boot-blacks violently toss him in and out of—a coat with a ripped lining in which Thurber invariably tangles himself—these are fundamentally George Smith and Mr. Monroe all over again. And so are the case histories that Thurber invents to confound such experts in mental efficiency and human relations as David Seabury (*How to Worry Successfully*), Dr. Louis Bisch (*Be Glad You're Neurotic*) and Dorothea Brande (*Wake Up and Live!*). The fearsome theorists, users of jargon as foolish as that used by Marxist literary critics in the thirties, cannot explain the sequences of motive and act that Thurber devises to prove how the undisciplined mind is better adapted to a confused world than one as streamlined as a machine. Yet, other pieces (short stories, most often) in both these volumes are controlled by a tone that more than counterbalances the humor.

This tone is perhaps most appropriately to be called melancholy, closer to dejection than to wistfulness. One of its earliest expressions precedes even *Is Sex Necessary?* In "Menaces in May" (1928) a middle-aged man whose wife has been gone a long time is made nostalgic by an evening encounter with a grammar-school sweetheart and her saxophone-loving husband. Wandering homeward through the gloom of New York City at three o'clock in the morning, he witnesses scenes of frustration, overhears ugly judgments, harsh threats, and the drunken mutterings of morose men thwarted in love and snoring in the subway. He goes to bed trying to think of his lovely Lydia amid echoes of vulgar realities. But in 1928 that story is something of an exception; in the late thirties its sense of defeat is a more frequent characteristic. In "Evening's at Seven" a middle-aged man's attempted affair is aborted by temperament and chance, and he goes home to his wife, with whom life is just habit. In "The Man on the Train" the narrator finds himself compellingly aware of and sympathetic with a fellow passenger who, the conductor later tells him, "just lost his little girl." In "One Is a Wanderer" another middle-aged man, whose only home is a hotel room next to that of another man like himself, remembers, analyzes, tries wearily to divert himself by staring at drugstore counters and visiting bars, and returns to his room to be ironically haunted by the words of "Bye, Bye, Blackbird": "Make my bed and light the light/For I'll be home late tonight. . . ." The concluding piece in *The Middle-Aged Man* describes the narrator's overpowering de-

sire to hide in a box. *Let Your Mind Alone* is a title with an unmistakable note of urgency. And the phrase "the Hiding Generation" is more than a flippant answer to women who might ask
Thurber at cocktail parties whether it is to the Lost Generation
that he belongs.

Possibly the point about Thurber's attitude is conclusively made
by noting how the somber tone operates when the story also has
possibilities for humor. "The Private Life of Mr. Bidwell" and
"The Breaking Up of the Winships" provide nice illustrations.
Both begin with marital discussions that are essentially trivial and
laughable, and conclude with marital dissolutions about which it
is impossible even to smile. Mr. Bidwell irritates his wife by hold-
ing his breath and multiplying numbers in his head until "the curious bond that held . . . [the Bidwells] together snapped. . . . The
thing was simply over."

> George Bidwell lives alone now (his wife remarried). He never
> goes to parties anymore, and his old circle of friends rarely sees
> him. The last time that any of them did see him, he was walking
> along a country road with the uncertain gait of a blind man: he
> was trying to see how many steps he could take without opening
> his eyes.

The Winships fall apart over an argument about the relative merits
of Greta Garbo and Donald Duck, and nothing anyone can do will
bring husband and wife together again; each adamantly identifies
his integrity with the position he has at first whimsically but ultimately fatally asserted.

The older generation had a vigorous humanity that encompassed
their oddities, but the Bidwells and Winships, and others who
might be listed, unhappily illustrate all that the phrase "the modern temper" has come to signify. Here is dehumanization in action.
Persons have no resources beyond their rituals and their nerves, or
their reflexes. Society becomes the graveyard of individuality, and
it is the man with ordinary feeling and simple compassion who
would appear eccentric in his ability to forsake detachment in the
face of another's pain. The old centers do not hold. Men and
women are being flung apart, atomized. The very thing that would
hold them together—conformity—is the one thing that takes no
account of them as persons. In short, what makes old-fashioned
eccentricity alone no answer is that in Thurber's time its corollary
may well be loneliness: it may be loneliness when society itself is
a mere form rather than a place for persons to exhibit what dis-

tinguishes one from another. If in *My Life and Hard Times* mis-understandings are funny, in the later stories they border on the tragic. And the worst aspect of it is that men and women, scarcely unconventional, fail to examine their habits and complacently spin along the disturbed orbit to disaster. The automatic response has superseded the purposeful commitment. Abstraction takes the place of experience, and class names obliterate the self. Persons have become indistinguishable from the little quanta that spot film plates. Appropriately, Thurber declares their isolation a sad rather than glad plight. Indeed, even if they were reflective people they would be defeated, for they would retire from a tawdry world into a hotel room, or seek a box to hide in.

Thurber, though, is clearly no misanthrope. One always feels that something worth recovering has been defeated; hence that recovery of this something is still a good. Man is not necessarily *all* destruction, but he is so *unless—*. This *unless—* is what distinguishes Thurber's preoccupation from 1939 onward; and a wonderful little story, "The Wood Duck," in *Let Your Mind Alone*, provides an unmistakable indication of the realm in which hope is to lie. In its opposition of inescapably symbolic details—especially between the graceful fowl and the speeding car that hits him—it celebrates all that can be contrasted to a mechanized life. On the one hand, the farmer, the men in the truck, the narrator and his wife, all feel that the wild duck confers a distinction on the farm he has adopted; on the other, the driver is unaware of, or at least indifferent to, the unspoiled beauty the machine has violated. When the duck flutters into the woods, something precious is lost; when he returns, he brings value into the institutional world. In the words of the narrator's wife near the end there is evidence of human gratitude for experiencing something close to nature. "I am glad he is [back] . . . ," she says. "I hated to think of him all alone out there in the woods." Even more important than the gratitude, though, there is here an understated awareness of the needs of men.

These needs clearly require a sense of what Thoreau called "the infinite state of our relations." The human being is lost when he loses his sense of his limitation, his mortality; when he equates the private with the absolute. Emerson could preach self-reliance because he had the oversoul in the offing; but Thurber's society has ignored the relationship and thereby denied both the self and the context for its being. Our only morality is embodied in our clichés. Heed their purveyors and be saved. *The Last Flower, a Parable in Pictures* (1939) and *Fables for Our Time and Famous Poems Illus-*

trated (1940) remind us how suicidal unself-critical man can be. The acceptance of empty forms is not only frustrating; it is utterly catastrophic. *The Last Flower* exhibits the disastrous course of human habits, the way men and women forget that their source and inspiration lie in what we may term nature—and the way that this forgetting allows mankind to become pretentious, arrogant and, finally, fatally warlike. The last, the best, the only hope is of earth itself: it is lodged in the natural cycle, the regenerative power of nature whose lone flower will seek invincibly to bloom again. The *Fables* makes this point in another way. Thurber simply turns Aesop about to examine the empty forms of words, platitudes, in the light of the life they are meant to describe. The animal world and the human world are compared to reveal the superiority of the animal. "If you do as humans do, it will be the end of you." The hen that shouts "The heavens are falling down" is not so foolish as everyone laughingly thinks. The heavens *do* fall; everyone *is* killed. And the narrator is not a bit surprised. Even the devastatingly funny illustrations of such famous poems as "Excelsior," "Lochinvar," "Locksley Hall," and "Barbara Frietchie" are presented to pose the question of what the poets' words *really* mean; the drawings are literal and thereby assail complacent imprecision. They are instructions in needed perspective.

The sense of relation that humanity needs is, thus, a sense of a saving connection with a primary spirit, something elemental that civilization disclaims at its peril. To disclaim this something is ultimately to deny the whole self. It is nothing less than this truth that Thurber and Elliott Nugent show Professor Tommy Turner in *The Male Animal* (1940). Before Turner can overcome the threats to his academic freedom and his marriage, he has to learn that there is something effete about not living any longer "in the days of King Arthur, when you fought for your woman. Nowadays," he notes, "the man and his wife and the other man talk it over. Quietly and calmly. They all go out to dinner together." They are, in short, the creatures of Reason, but so sophisticated as to be drained of anything to be reasonable about. What human beings have forgotten is that "we are male animals, too"—like tigers, wolves, sea lions, land crabs and birds of paradise. But the lesson is not simply to affirm the nakedly primitive. (Compare William Inge's *Picnic* and some of Tennessee Williams' plays.) Turner is, after all, always the embodiment of thought and imagination, the man capable of asserting the freedom to think as one will; the memorable drinking scene even underscores this, for were he to come to his illumination in a moment of sober reflection the words of the lesson would be left with only their face value, but instead, the hilarity of the occasion is part of the argument: the very order of illustrations, from tiger to sea lion (who "roars with his antlers") and finally to crab and bird of paradise, is a qualification produced by wit testifying to the superiority of mind over mere impulse. It is analysis without feeling, without passionate commitment, that is condemned. "A woman likes a man who does something," Turner declares. "All male animals fight for the female. . . . They don't just sit and talk. They act." What the play finally argues, then, is that the good life lies in recovering a certain principle of action, in establishing a source for responses that can make those responses trustworthy. Over-refinement and intellectualism can reduce persons to a level on which their problems are capable of solution by tranquilizers. The fact is, Thurber states elsewhere, "that the bare foot of Man has been too long away from the living earth, that . . . [Man] has been too busy with the construction of engines, which are, of all the things on earth, the farthest removed from the shape and intention of nature."

Emphasis is given to Thurber's desire to re-establish a relation between man and "the shape and intention of nature" by his turning in the early forties to the writing of fairly tales. Momentarily freed of the data of a machine-scarred earth, especially at a time when dreadful war is an actuality, Thurber is able to make his point in an affirmative tone scarcely appropriate in a less fanciful form. It is an injustice to Thurber's art not to analyze in detail the rich texture of *Many Moons* (1943), *The Great Quillow* (1944) and *The White Deer* (1945); in the last especially, the playful language, the simultaneous use and parody of the fairy tale genre, the nice tension between humor and gravity deserve, for their own sake, full treatment to show how Thurber's form becomes itself a statement. But it will have to be sufficient for present purposes to mention that the conflicts and contrasts in these tales are familiar ones: materialism opposed to art; exaggerated gravity, to laughter; worldliness, to provincial innocence; practicality, to dreaminess. By subtly and wittily introducing a modern point of view, Thurber makes clear that the fairy tale is itself something of an act of faith in the innocence and purity that fairy tales usually celebrate. At the same time, the fact of that intrusion also declares that it is a large awareness rather than an immature belief that is at work. Little princesses, toy makers, musicians and poets are closer to sensing the shape and intention of nature—closer to exhibiting its virtues, for

that matter—than are the royal mathematicians, village council-
men, mighty hunters and other materialists who pride themselves
on their mastery of the physical world. But it is, after all, awareness
of that fact that is the final value, and that awareness is the prop-
erty of a mature and humble mind that encompasses the ability to
believe quite as much as it does the ability to act.

This special perspective leaves many questions to be answered.
Some of them appear in variously shaded guises in the other writing that Thurber has done since the year of *The Last Flower*, 1939,
when "The Secret Life of Walter Mitty" may be said to usher in
the major period. As ever, Thurber is trying to find a realm where
the individual can maintain his self; and as ever, too, there seems
to be no answer without qualifications—an appropriate enough
way of assaulting rigid forms. Yet there is ultimately what has already been suggested, a humanistic affirmation. Of course, at no
time does Thurber forsake one kind of writing and immerse himself exclusively in another. Although there may be no *My Life and
Hard Times*, there are still instances of great humor, more fairy
tales and fables. But most of them are marked by the increasing
complexity and depth that are best embodied in such important
and challenging masterpieces as "The Secret Life of Walter Mitty"
(1939), "The Whip-Poor-Will" (1941), "The Catbird Seat" (1942),
"The Cane in the Corridor" (1943), "A Friend of the Earth" (1949),
"Teacher's Pet" (1949) and *The Thirteen Clocks* (1950).

Among the most successful protagonists in these stories are Walter Mitty and Erwin Martin (of "The Catbird Seat"), both of whom
win not too dissimilar victories over the commonplace, the dead
level of practicality, the enemies of the imagination. A definition
of the character of these victories suggests their meaning. When
Mitty faces the firing squad, "erect and motionless, proud and dis-
dainful, Walter Mitty the Undefeated, inscrutable to the last," the
victory has its limits. It is not only private—one that cannot give
him a place in society; it is ridden by the clichés of pulp romances
and Grade C movies. Nonetheless, it is a victory, even if qualified,
that contributes to self-preservation. Mr. Martin, whose stature is
greater insofar as he does bear real arms against his sea of troubles,
likewise wins substantially and privately. By perceiving the thin
line between humor and pathos, absurdity and terror, that is reflected in the details, point of view and very tone of the story, he
is able to make his usual ineffectualness unusually effectual; Ulgine
Barrows, the threat to his sensibilities and his status, is ironically
defeated. But even as he, by actual act, gives genuine dignity to

those sensibilities and that status, it is clear that both the cause and the reward of his success must be isolation. His employer does not truly understand either Mrs. Barrows or Mr. Martin, and Mr. Martin can never enjoy his accomplishment except in private. Although he can never be again what he once was, he has to appear to others unchanged. Irony and cross-purposes must be the order of the day. This, though, is in part Mr. Martin's insight. He exploits the relationships of strangers and, like Walter Mitty, saves something worth saving: he saves, indeed, the inner life itself, the life that is not to be harnessed like the atom, streamlined like a spaceship, manipulated, calculated, fed to Univac; he saves the very seat of the self that is the universe—the realm that makes it possible to say, as was said some centuries ago, that the unexamined life is not worth living.

Mitty and Martin, and especially Martin, who after all *does* more than Mitty, are then an impressive distance from the eccentrics of *My Life and Hard Times* and the lonely wanderers and frustrates of *The Middle-Aged Man* and *Let Your Mind Alone*. They bear, generally speaking, the marks of solider affirmations.

The others of these stories dramatize complementary statements. In probing into recesses of the inner life, "The Whip-Poor-Will" and "The Cane in the Corridor" show how inadequate is the understanding of standardized minds; "The Whip-Poor-Will" especially, the more compelling of the two, demonstrates in the state trooper's dull comment ("Take more'n a whip-poor-will to cause a mess like that") that there is a whole life that minds enslaved by formulas do not, cannot, know. In commemorating the independence and victory of "a lazy rustic philosopher" in a test of repartee with a representative of the sophisticated world of urban wit and timetables, "A Friend of the Earth" both elevates the more natural man and, by making him superior in the realm of mind, elaborates upon some of the implications of *The Male Animal*; linking mind, nature and individuality, it receives confirmation of its emphasis from the gallery of portraits begun at the same time, *The Thurber Album* (1952), which recalls the solidity of pioneers who act rather than talk, who make their own world by relying on their strong inner resources, and who, guilty of no pretenses and conceiving of no age of suspicion like Thurber's, live in a period when the individual has not yet "taken on the gray color of the mass" but "each [possesses] . . . his own bright and separate values." Finally, in celebrating not only fantasy but laughter, Thurber's fourth fairy tale, *The Thirteen Clocks,* affirms the perspective that makes confidence in separate values possible without breeding smugness. For laughter, humanity's best means of exhibiting a sense of proportion, is the Duke's undoing and is the sound that echoes through the castle at the last.

A respect for nature, for action, for the inner life, for mind—it is a single complex, inseparable from what we mean by the sense of proportion that is to help the individual know his predicament. "Teacher's Pet," one of Thurber's most intense stories, provides, perhaps, a succinct concluding insight into the individual's essential situation. When the reflective, brooding Kelby, in a fury of self-accusation, hits the little boy who, bullied and afraid, reminds him of his own boyhood predicament and cowardice, he is ironically taken for a bully by the boy's father. And when the father tells a mutual friend, "I've seen some bullies in my time, but I never saw anything to match that," the friend puffs thoughtfully on a cigarette and says: "You never know about a man, Reynolds. You just never know."

This is the nub of it. And because it is, there are a variety of social implications. Not the least is the necessity for a structure in which the human mystery is secure, in which action can be more than bare reaction, in which individuals are respected as ends and not exploited as means, whether by political dictators or social relations experts. Or slogan writers. For the very use of language is related to the argument in behalf of individuality and the sense of relation. Insofar as perceptions are verbalized, words must be precise, sharp, telling. Whether employing an arresting metaphor or playfully juxtaposing the trite and the fresh, or simply inveighing against jargon, "polysyllabic monstrosititis," Thurber is warring for meaning—and for the only mind for whom that objective can make sense. It is fitting that his latest tale, *The Wonderful O,* should argue the value not only of love and hope and valor, but also of freedom; and it is equally fitting that he identifies the threat to freedom with an assault on language, on communication.

The Wonderful O is a singular mélange, to be sure. It is part somber romance, part parody of adventure stories, part prose, part rime, part allegory, part ridicule of the experts, part dream. The mingling of genres and inevitable complexity of tone make it impossible to accept the lesson smugly. If cocksureness were a danger, however, Thurber's recent collection of *Further Fables for Our Time* (1956) would chasten. The concluding fable tells of a scholarly lemming who refuses to join his fellow lemmings in their excited exodus to the sea. Although some imagine that the world is coming to an end and others believe it is a treasure hunt, and some expect salvation and others fear damnation, the scholar knows better; his studies long ago have told him that there is no devil in the forest or gems in the sea. He simply shakes his head sorrowfully, tears up all he has written about the species, and starts his studies all over again. "All men," the moral reads, "should strive to learn before they die what they are running from, and to, and why."

To attribute to man the ability both so to learn and then to act in consequence is almost to pay him the tribute that painters represent with the halo—almost but not quite—and yet better—because ordinary men are more complex than the saints.

James Thurber's Dream Book

by Malcolm Cowley

There are two ways to review the selected writings and drawings of James Thurber. The wrong way, I think, is to be deeply
impressed by the fact that Thurber is a funny man and try to
match his book with a funny review, making great use of exaggera-
tion and overstatements, which you have been taught to regard as
the essence of American humor. The other and somewhat revolutionary method is the one I should like to follow. It consists in reviewing his book exactly as if it were the work of any other skillful
and serious American writer.

The Thurber Carnival contains thirty-three of his "pieces," a
general term to describe his stories, almost-stories, light essays and
autobiographical sketches. All but one of them first appeared in the
New Yorker. Most of them have also appeared in one or another
of his earlier volumes, but the first six were previously uncollected.
In addition to the pieces, there is "My Life and Hard Times," complete with illustrations; and the selection ends with 125 pages of
Thurber's drawings. These suffer from being reduced to a maxi-
mum width of four inches; they sometimes lose the effect of movement and part of the detail gets blurred (as note "Zero Hour—
Connecticut" and "Gettysburg" on pages 366–67); but it is good
to have so many of them together, even if we have to look at them
through a reading glass. The pieces are intact, and they are just as
funny or sad or frightening as when we read them the first time.

Most of them might have been written to illustrate the difference between wit and humor. Wit, says the *Shorter Oxford*, is "that
quality of speech or writing which consists in the apt association
of thought and expression, calculated to surprise by its unexpected-
ness; later always with ref. to the utterance of brilliant or sparkling
things in an amusing way." Humor, says *Webster's Collegiate*, "im-

plies, commonly, broader human sympathies than wit, and a more
kindly sense of the incongruous, often blended with pathos." There
is not much wit in Thurber's writing, although there is plenty of
it in his conversation. Occasionally in a story he permits himself
a relatively brilliant or sparkling metaphor—he says, for example,
"This midsummer Saturday had got off to a sulky start, and now,
at three in the afternoon, it sat, sticky and restive, on our laps";
but for the most part he confines himself to the almost businesslike
description of incongruous situations that are often blended with
pathos.

He doesn't always bother to be funny. Eight of the pieces, by
my count, are quite serious in effect and intention, and several of
the others balance on the edge between farce and disaster, like a
clown on a very high trapeze. Four of them—all funny ones—end
with the murder of the hero, and two—both serious—end with his
natural death (one of these last heroes is a dog). Four others end
with dreams of killing or being killed, and two with the hero of one
and the villainess of the other reduced to raving madness. There
are fifteen pieces—almost half the selections in the book—that are
largely based on nightmares, hallucinations or elaborate and cruel
practical jokes. Entering Thurber's middle-class world is like wandering into a psychiatric ward and not being quite sure whether
you are a visitor or an inmate. The author himself bustles around
in a white jacket, but sometimes he stops to say in a pleasant, matter-of-fact voice, "You know, they don't suspect. They think I'm a
doctor."

He writes so naturally and conversationally that it is hard to
realize how much work goes into his stories. His art is in fact extremely conscious, and it is based on a wide knowledge of contemporary writing. In a letter to Fred B. Millett, written in 1939,
Thurber listed some of his favorite authors: Henry James first of
all, then Conrad Aiken, Hemingway, Fitzgerald, Edmund Wilson
and Willa Cather, among others. The list would indicate, he said,
"that I like the perfectly done, the well ordered, as against the
sprawling chunk of life. . . . I also owe a debt to E. B. White . . .
whose perfect clarity of expression is it seems to me equaled by very
few and surpassed by simply nobody. . . . I came to the *New Yorker*
a writer of journalese and it was my study of White's writing, I
think, that helped me to straighten out my prose so that people
could see what it meant." Besides learning to write with an easy
flow and coherence that very few authors achieve, he also learned
to omit everything inessential, including the winks, the ribnudgings

and the philosophical remarks of older American humorists. He achieves a sort of costly simplicity, like that of well tailored clothes or good conversation.

Within his fixed limits of length and sympathy and subject, one feels almost nothing but admiration for Thurber's work; one's only regret is that he hasn't made the limits broader. Other things being equal, a good long story is better than a good short one; and most of Thurber's begin and end within 3,000 words, a convenient length for the *New Yorker*. Most of his characters are upper-middle-class couples from the upper Middle West, who have moved to New York, prospered financially and bought or rented houses in Connecticut. His favorite subject is their domestic quarrels, which he portrayed in a famous series of drawings . . . as "The War Between Men and Women."

Henry James in his time was also impressed by the conflict between American business or professional men and their wives. In *The American Scene,* he described it as "a queer deep split or chasm between the two stages of personal polish, the two levels of the conversible state, at which the sexes have arrived." It was the wives who had reached what he regarded as the much higher level. "Nothing," he said, "is more concomitantly striking than the fact that the women, over the land—allowing for every element of exception—appear to be of a markedly finer texture than the men." He recommended the subject to the painter of manners, and Thurber has adopted it as his own. When he describes the split or chasm, however, it is as if each of the sexes had crossed to the opposite side. The women in his stories are hard, logical, aggressive; they have all the virtues and vices that James assigned to businessmen. The husbands, on the other hand, are widely read, dreamy, introspective; they are helpless without their wives, but at the same time they try to escape into an imagined world of men. Thus Walter Mitty, driving the family car, pictures himself as the commander of a huge, hurtling eight-engined navy hydroplane. He imagines the crew looking up and grinning as a storm beats against the wings. "The Old Man'll get us through," they say to one another. "The Old Man ain't afraid of Hell!" . . . "Not so fast! You're driving too fast," says Mrs. Mitty; and the hydroplane of Walter Mitty's dream comes hurtling down.

Almost all of Thurber's heroes are dreamers and escapists, even when they are happily married. The author defends them in his illustrated "Fables for Our Time." The moral of one fable is, "Who flies afar from the sphere of our sorrow is here today and here to-

morrow"; of another, "Run, don't walk, to the nearest desert island." In his autobiographical sketches, Thurber describes two easy
methods for escaping into a fantastic world: by sound and by sight.
The first method consists in misunderstanding or misinterpreting
words and phrases. Thus, he hears a station agent repeating time
and again over the telephone, "Conductor Reagan on the 142 has
the lady the office was asking about"; and soon, brooding over the
sentence, he imagines himself among silky, desperate spies. On another occasion his maid, who always mispronounces words, comes
to his study and says, "They are here with the reeves." His hired
man, who has the same bad habit, tells him, "I go hunt grotches in
de voods," and again, "We go to the garrick now and become
warbs." The servants are referring to wreaths and crotches and
wasps in the garret; but before Thurber succeeds in unraveling
their remarks, they have sent him wandering off into surrealist
landscapes that he compares, at one point, to the secret world of
Salvador Dali.

His other means of escape is simply by taking off his glasses. Because his vision is defective, the whole world thereupon assumes a
different shape for him. On one such occasion, so he says, "I saw
the Cuban flag flying over a national bank, I saw a gay old lady
with a gray parasol walk right through the side of a truck, I saw a
cat roll across a street in a small striped barrel, I saw bridges rise
lazily into the air, like balloons." Reading these lines, and the rest
of "The Admiral on the Wheel," one can scarcely help thinking
of a famous passage from Rimbaud's "Alchemy of the Word":

> I habituated myself to simple hallucination: I would see quite
> honestly a mosque instead of a factory, a school of drummers com-
> posed of angels, barouches on the roads of the sky, a drawingroom
> at the bottom of a lake: monsters, mysteries; the announcement of a
> musical comedy would cause horrors to rise before me.
> Then I explained my magical sophistries by the hallucination of
> words!
> I ended by finding sacred the disorder of my mind.

There is in fact a curious similarity between one type of fantastic
American humor and the current in European poetry that is represented in various phases by Rimbaud and Lautréamont, by expres-
sionism, dadaism and surrealism. None of these schools has flourished here (although surrealism now has more disciples than the
others possessed), and I think the reason may be that our sense of
rightness is offended when we hear a young man proclaiming that

he has a wild, satanic imagination whose disorder he finds sacred, and then describing his dreams. But the truth is that we enjoy fantasy much more than the French; and we gladly listen to the same type of dreams when they are described by Thurber in a matter-of-fact voice and with a self-deprecatory air.

Thurber on Himself

an interview by George Plimpton and Max Steele

The Hôtel Continental, just down from the Place Vendôme on the Rue Castiglione. It is from here that Janet Flanner (Genêt) sends her Paris letter to *The New Yorker,* and it is here that the Thurbers usually stay while in Paris. "We like it because the service is first-rate without being snobbish."

Thurber was standing to greet us in a small salon whose cold European formality had been somewhat softened and warmed by well-placed vases of flowers, by stacks and portable shelves of American novels in bright dust jackets, and by pads of yellow paper and bouquets of yellow pencils on the desk. Thurber impresses one immediately by his physical size. After years of delighting in the shy, trapped little man in the Thurber cartoons and the confused and bewildered man who has fumbled in and out of some of the funniest books written in this century, we, perhaps like many readers, were expecting to find the frightened little man in person. Not at all. Thurber by his firm handgrasp and confident voice and by the way he lowered himself into his chair gave the impression of outward calmness and assurance. Though his eyesight has almost failed him, it is not a disability which one is aware of for more than the opening minute, and if Thurber seems to be the most nervous person in the room, it is because he has learned to put his visitors so completely at ease.

He talks in a surprisingly boyish voice, which is flat with the accents of the Midwest where he was raised and, though slow in tempo, never dull. He is not an easy man to pin down with questions. He prefers to sidestep them and, rather than instructing, he entertains with a vivid series of anecdotes and reminiscences.

Opening the interview with a long history of the bloodhound,

"Thurber on Himself" (editor's title). From George Plimpton and Max Steele, "James Thurber," interview with George Plimpton and Max Steele in *Writers at Work: The Paris Review Interviews,* First Series, Malcolm Cowley, ed. (New York: The Viking Press, 1959). Copyright © 1957, 1958 by The Paris Review, Inc. All rights reserved. Reprinted by permission of The Viking Press, Inc. and Martin Secker & Warburg Limited.

Thurber was only with some difficulty persuaded to shift to a discussion of his craft. Here again his manner was typical—the anecdotes, the reminiscences punctuated with direct quotes and factual data. His powers of memory are astounding. In quoting anyone—perhaps a conversation of a dozen years before—Thurber pauses slightly, his voice changes in tone, and you know what you're hearing is exactly as it was said.

THURBER: Well, you know it's a nuisance—to have memory like mine—as well as an advantage. It's . . . well . . . like a whore's top drawer. There's so much else in there that's junk—costume jewelry, unnecessary telephone numbers whose exchanges no longer exist. For instance, I can remember the birthday of anybody who's ever told me his birthday. Dorothy Parker—August 22, Lewis Gannett—October 3, Andy White—July 9, Mrs. White —September 17. I can go on with about two hundred. So can my mother. She can tell you the birthday of the girl I was in love with in the third grade, in 1903. Offhand, just like that. I got my powers of memory from her. Sometimes it helps out in the most extraordinary way. You remember Robert M. Coates? Bob Coates? He is the author of *The Eater of Darkness*, which Ford Madox Ford called the first true Dadaist novel. Well, the week after Stephen Vincent Benét died—Coates and I had both known him—we were talking about Benét. Coates was trying to remember an argument he had had with Benét some fifteen years before. He couldn't remember. I said, "I can." Coates told me that was impossible since I hadn't been there. "Well," I said, "you happened to mention it in passing about twelve years ago. You were arguing about a play called *Swords*." I was right, and Coates was able to take it up from there. But it's strange to reach a position where your friends have to be supplied with their own memories. It's bad enough dealing with your own.

INTERVIEWERS: Still, it must be a great advantage for the writer. I don't suppose you have to take notes.

THURBER: No. I don't have to do the sort of thing Fitzgerald did with *The Last Tycoon*—the voluminous, the tiny and meticulous notes, the long descriptions of character. I can keep all these things in my mind. I wouldn't have to write down "three roses in a vase" or something, or a man's middle name. Henry James dictated notes just the way that I write. His note writing was part of the creative act, which is why his prefaces are so good. He dictated notes to see what it was they might come to.

INTERVIEWERS: Then you don't spend much time prefiguring your work?

THURBER: No. I don't bother with charts and so forth. Elliott Nugent, on the other hand, is a careful constructor. When we were working on *The Male Animal* together, he was constantly concerned with plotting the play. He could plot the thing from back to front—what was going to happen here, what sort of situation would end the first-act curtain, and so forth. I can't work that way. Nugent would say, "Well, Thurber, we've got our problem, we've got all these people in the living room. Now what are we going to do with them?" I'd say that I didn't know and couldn't tell him until I'd sat down at the typewriter and found out. I don't believe the writer should know too much where he's going. If he does, he runs into old man blueprint—old man propaganda.

INTERVIEWERS: Is the act of writing easy for you?

THURBER: For me it's mostly a question of rewriting. It's part of a constant attempt on my part to make the finished version smooth, to make it seem effortless. A story I've been working on—"The Train on Track Six," it's called—was rewritten fifteen complete times. There must have been close to 240,000 words in all the manuscripts put together, and I must have spent two thousand hours working at it. Yet the finished version can't be more than twenty thousand words.

INTERVIEWERS: Then it's rare that your work comes out right the first time?

THURBER: Well, my wife took a look at the first version of something I was doing not long ago and said, "Goddamn it, Thurber, that's high-school stuff." I have to tell her to wait until the seventh draft, it'll work out all right. I don't know why that should be so, that the first or second draft of everything I write reads as if it was turned out by a charwoman. I've only written one piece quickly. I wrote a thing called "File and Forget" in one afternoon—but only because it was a series of letters just as one would ordinarily dictate. And I'd have to admit that the last letter of the series, after doing all the others that one afternoon, took me a week. It was the end of the piece and I had to fuss over it.

INTERVIEWERS: Does the fact that you're dealing with humor slow down the production?

THURBER: It's possible. With humor you have to look out for traps. You're likely to be very gleeful with what you've first put down, and you think it's fine, very funny. One reason you go over and over it is to make the piece sound less as if you were having a lot of fun with it yourself. You try to play it down. In fact, if there's such a thing as a *New Yorker* style, that would be it—playing it down.

INTERVIEWERS: Do you envy those who write at high speed, as against your method of constant revision?

THURBER: Oh, no, I don't, though I do admire their luck. Hervey Allen, you know, the author of the big best-seller *Anthony Adverse*, seriously told a friend of mine who was working on a biographical piece on Allen that he could close his eyes, lie down on a bed, and hear the voices of his ancestors. Furthermore there was some sort of angel-like creature that danced along his pen while he was writing. He wasn't balmy by any means. He just felt he was in communication with some sort of metaphysical recorder. So you see the novelists have all the luck. I never knew a humorist who got any help from his ancestors. Still, the act of writing is either something the writer dreads or actually likes, and I actually like it. Even rewriting's fun. You're getting somewhere, whether it seems to move or not. I remember Elliot Paul and I used to argue about rewriting back in 1925 when we both worked for the *Chicago Tribune* in Paris. It was his conviction you should leave the story as it came out of the typewriter, no changes. Naturally, he worked fast. Three novels he could turn out, each written in three weeks' time. I remember once he came into the office and said that a sixty-thousand-word manuscript had been stolen. No carbons existed, no notes. We were all horrified. But it didn't bother him at all. He'd just get back to the typewriter and bat away again. But for me—writing as fast as that would seem too facile. Like my drawings, which I do very quickly, sometimes so quickly that the result is an accident, something I hadn't intended at all. People in the arts I've run into in France are constantly indignant when I say I'm a writer and not an artist. They tell me I mustn't run down my drawings. I try to explain that I do them for relaxation, and that I do them too fast for them to be called art.

INTERVIEWERS: You say that your drawings often don't come out the way you intended?

THURBER: Well, once I did a drawing for *The New Yorker* of a naked woman on all fours up on top of a bookcase—a big bookcase. She's up there near the ceiling, and in the room are her husband and two other women. The husband is saying to one of the women, obviously a guest, "This is the present Mrs. Harris. That's my first wife up there." Well, when I did the cartoon originally

I meant the naked woman to be at the top of a flight of stairs, but I lost the sense of perspective and instead of getting in the stairs when I drew my line down, there she was stuck up there, naked, on a bookcase.

Incidentally, that cartoon really threw *The New Yorker* editor, Harold Ross. He approached any humorous piece of writing, or more particularly a drawing, not only grimly but realistically. He called me on the phone and asked if the woman up on the bookcase was supposed to be alive, stuffed, or dead. I said, "I don't know, but I'll let you know in a couple of hours." After a while I called him back and told him I'd just talked to my taxidermist, who said you can't stuff a woman, that my doctor had told me a dead woman couldn't support herself on all fours. "So, Ross," I said, "she must be alive." "Well then," he said, "what's she doing up there naked in the home of her husband's second wife?" I told him he had me there.

INTERVIEWERS: But he published it.

THURBER: Yes, he published it, growling a bit. He had a fine understanding of humor, Ross, though he couldn't have told you about it. When I introduced Ross to the work of Peter de Vries, he first said, "He won't be good; he won't be funny; he won't know English." (He was the only successful editor I've known who approached everything like a ship going on the rocks.) But when Ross had looked at the work he said, "How can you get this guy on the phone?" He couldn't have said why, but he had that bloodhound instinct. The same with editing. He was a wonderful man at detecting something wrong with a story without knowing why.

INTERVIEWERS: Could he develop a writer?

THURBER: Not really. It wasn't true what they often said of him— that he broke up writers like matches—but still he wasn't the man to develop a writer. He was an unread man. Well, he'd read Mark Twain's *Life on the Mississippi* and several other books he told me about—medical books—and he took the Encyclopedia Britannica to the bathroom with him. I think he was about up to H when he died. But still his effect on writers was considerable. When you first met him you couldn't believe he was the editor of *The New Yorker* and afterward you couldn't believe that anyone else could have been. The main thing he was interested in was clarity. Someone once said of *The New Yorker* that it never contained a sentence that would puzzle an intelligent fourteen-year-old or in any way affect her morals badly. Ross didn't like that, but nevertheless he was a purist and perfectionist and it had a tremendous effect on all of us: it kept us from being sloppy. When I first met him he asked me if I knew English. I thought he meant French or a foreign language. But he repeated, "Do you know English?" When I said I did he replied, "Goddamn it, nobody knows English." As Andy White mentioned in his obituary, Ross approached the English sentence as though it was an enemy, something that was going to throw him. He used to fuss for an hour over a comma. He'd call me in for lengthy discussions about the Thurber colon. And as for poetic license, he'd say, "Damn any license to get things wrong." In fact, Ross read so carefully that often he didn't get the sense of your story. I once said: "I wish you'd read my stories for pleasure, Ross." He replied he hadn't time for that.

INTERVIEWERS: It's strange that one of the main ingredients of humor—low comedy—has never been accepted for *The New Yorker*.

THURBER: Ross had a neighbor woman's attitude about it. He never got over his Midwestern provincialism. His idea was that sex is an incident. "If you can prove it," I said, "we can get it in a box on the front page of *The New York Times*." Now I don't want to say that in private life Ross was a prude. But as regards the theater or the printed page he certainly was. For example, he once sent an office memorandum to us in a sealed envelope. It was an order: "When you send me a memorandum with four-letter words in it, *seal it*. There are women in this office." I said, "Yah, Ross, and they know a lot more of these words than you do." When women were around he was very conscious of them. Once my wife and I were in his office and Ross was discussing a man and woman he knew much better than we did. Ross told us, "I have every rearon to believe that they're *s-l-e-e-p-i-n-g* together." My wife replied, "Why, Harold Ross, what words you do spell out." But honest to goodness, that was genuine. Women are either good or bad, he once told me, and the good ones must not hear these things.

Incidentally, I'm telling these things to refresh my memory. I'm doing a short book on him called "Ross in Charcoal." I'm putting a lot of this stuff in. People may object, but after all it's a portrait of the man and I see no reason for not putting it in.

INTERVIEWERS: Did he have much direct influence on your own work?

THURBER: After the seven years I spent in newspaper writing, it was more E. B. White who taught me about writing, how to clear up sloppy journalese. He was a strong influence, and for a long time in the beginning I thought he might be too much of one. But at least he got me away from a rather curious style I was starting to perfect—tight journalese laced with heavy doses of Henry James.

INTERVIEWERS: Henry James was a strong influence, then?

THURBER: I have the reputation for having read all of Henry James. Which would argue a misspent youth *and* middle age.

INTERVIEWERS: But there were things to be learned from him?

THURBER: Yes, but again he was an influence you had to get over. Especially if you wrote for *The New Yorker*. Harold Ross wouldn't have understood it. I once wrote a piece called "The Beast in the Dingle" which everybody took as a parody. Actually it was a conscious attempt to write the story as James would have written it. Ross looked at it and said: "Goddamn it, this is too literary; I got only fifteen per cent of the allusions." My wife and I often tried to figure out which were the fifteen per cent he could have got.

You know, I've occasionally wondered what James would have done with our world. I've just written a piece—"Preface to Old Friends," it's called—in which James at the age of a hundred and four writes a preface to a novel about our age in which he summarizes the trends and complications, but at the end is so completely lost he doesn't really care enough to read it over to find his way out again.

That's the trouble with James. You get bored with him finally. He lived in the time of four-wheelers, and no bombs, and the problems then seemed a bit special and separate. That's one reason you feel restless reading him. James is like—well, I had a bulldog once who used to drag rails around, enormous ones—six-, eight-, twelve-foot rails. He loved to get them in the middle and you'd hear him growling out there, trying to bring the thing home. Once he brought home a chest of drawers—without the drawers in it. Found it on an ash-heap. Well, he'd start to get these things in the garden gate, everything finely balanced, you see, and then *crash*, he'd come up against the gate posts. He'd get it through finally, but I had that feeling in some of the James novels: that he was trying to get that rail through a gate not wide enough for it.

INTERVIEWERS: How about Mark Twain? Pretty much everybody believes him to have been the major influence on American humorists.

THURBER: Everybody wants to know if I've learned from Mark Twain. Actually I've never read much of him. I did buy *Tom Sawyer*, but dammit, I'm sorry, I've not got around to reading it all the way through. I told H. L. Mencken that, and he was shocked. He said America had produced only two fine novels: *Huck Finn* and *Babbitt*. Of course it's always a matter of personal opinion—these lists of the great novels. I can remember calling on Frank Harris —he was about seventy then—when I was on the *Chicago Tribune*'s edition in Nice. In his house he had three portraits on the wall—Mark Twain, Frank Harris, and I think it was Hawthorne. Harris was in the middle. Harris would point up to them and say, "Those three are the best American writers. The one in the middle is the best." Harris really thought he was wonderful. Once he told me he was going to live to be a hundred. When I asked him what the formula was, he told me it was very simple. He said, "I've bought myself a stomach pump and one half-hour after dinner I pump myself out." Can you imagine that? Well, it didn't work. It's a wonder it didn't kill him sooner.

INTERVIEWERS: Could we ask you why you've never attempted a long work?

THURBER: I've never wanted to write a long work. Many writers feel a sense of frustration or something if they haven't, but I don't.

INTERVIEWERS: Perhaps the fact that you're writing humor imposes a limit on the length of a work.

THURBER: Possibly. But brevity in any case—whether the work is supposed to be humorous or not—would seem to me to be desirable. Most of the books I like are short books: *The Red Badge of Courage, The Turn of the Screw,* Conrad's short stories, *A Lost Lady,* Joseph Hergesheimer's *Wild Oranges,* Victoria Lincoln's *February Hill, The Great Gatsby. . . .* You know Fitzgerald once wrote Thomas Wolfe: "You're a putter-inner and I'm a taker-outer." I stick with Fitzgerald. I don't believe, as Wolfe did, that you have to turn out a massive work before being judged a writer. Wolfe once told me at a cocktail party I didn't know what it was to be a writer. My wife, standing next to me, complained about that. "But my husband *is* a writer," she said. Wolfe was genuinely surprised. "He is?" he asked. "Why, all I ever see is that stuff of his in *The New Yorker.*" In other words, he felt that prose under five thousand words was certainly not the work of a writer . . . it was some kind of doodling in words. If you said you were a writer, he wanted to know where the books were, the great big long books. He was really genuine about that.

I was interested to see William Faulkner's list not so long ago of the five most important American authors of this century. According to him Wolfe was first, Faulkner second—let's see, now that Wolfe's dead that puts Faulkner up there in the lead, doesn't it?—Dos Passos third, then Hemingway, and finally Steinbeck. It's interesting that the first three are putter-inners. They write expansive novels.

INTERVIEWERS: Wasn't Faulkner's criterion whether or not the author dared to go out on a limb?

THURBER: It seems to me you're going out on a limb these days to keep a book short.

INTERVIEWERS: Though you've never done a long serious work you have written stories—"The Cane in the Corridor" and "The Whippoorwill" in particular—in which the mood is far from humorous.

THURBER: In anything funny you write that isn't close to serious you've missed something along the line. But in those stories of which you speak there was an element of anger—something I wanted to get off my chest. I wrote "The Whippoorwill" after five eye operations. It came somewhere out of a grim fear in the back of my mind. I've never been able to trace it.

INTERVIEWERS: Some critics think that much of your work can be traced to the depicting of trivia as a basis for humor. In fact, there's been some criticism—

THURBER: Which is trivia—the diamond or the elephant? Any humorist must be interested in trivia, in every little thing that occurs in a household. It's what Robert Benchley did so well—in fact so well that one of the greatest fears of the humorous writer is that he has spent three weeks writing something done faster and better by Benchley in 1919. Incidently, you never got very far talking to Benchley about humor. He'd do a take-off of Max Eastman's *Enjoyment of Laughter*. "We must understand," he'd say, "that all sentences which begin with W are funny."

INTERVIEWERS: Would you care to define humor in terms of your own work?

THURBER: Well, someone once wrote a definition of the difference between English and American humor. I wish I could remember his name. I thought his definition very good. He said that the English treat the commonplace as if it were remarkable and the Americans treat the remarkable as if it were commonplace. I believe that's true of humorous writing. Years ago we did a parody of *Punch* in which Benchley did a short piece depicting a wife bursting into a room and shouting "The primroses are in bloom!"—treating the commonplace as remarkable, you see. In "The Secret

Life of Walter Mitty" I tried to treat the remarkable as common-place.

INTERVIEWERS: Does it bother you to talk about the stories on which you're working? It bothers many writers, though it would seem that particularly the humorous story is polished through retelling.

THURBER: Oh, yes. I often tell them at parties and places. And I write them there too.

INTERVIEWERS: You write them?

THURBER: I never quite know when I'm not writing. Sometimes my wife comes up to me at a party and says, "Dammit, Thurber, stop writing." She usually catches me in the middle of a paragraph. Or my daughter will look up from the dinner table and ask, "Is he sick?" "No," my wife says, "he's writing something." I have to do it that way on account of my eyes. I still write occasionally—in the proper sense of the word—using black crayon on yellow paper and getting perhaps twenty words to the page. My usual method, though, is to spend the mornings turning over the text in my mind. Then in the afternoon, between two and five, I call in a secretary and dictate to her. I can do about two thousand words. It took me about ten years to learn.

INTERVIEWERS: How about the new crop of writers? Do you note any good humorists coming along with them?

THURBER: There don't seem to be many coming up. I once had a psychoanalyst tell me that the depression had a considerable effect—much worse than Hitler and the war. It's a tradition for a child to see his father in uniform as something glamorous—not his father coming home from Wall Street in a three-button sack suit saying, "We're ruined," and the mother bursting into tears—a catastrophe that to a child's mind is unexplainable. There's been a great change since the thirties. In those days students used to ask me what Peter Arno did at night. And about Dorothy Parker. Now they want to know what my artistic credo is. An element of interest seems to have gone out of them.

INTERVIEWERS: Has the shift in the mood of the times had any effect on your own work?

THURBER: Well, *The Thurber Album* was written at a time when in America there was a feeling of fear and suspicion. It's quite different from *My Life and Hard Times,* which was written earlier and is a funnier and better book. The *Album* was kind of an escape—going back to the Middle West of the last century and the beginning of this, when there wasn't this fear and hysteria. I wanted to write the story of some solid American characters, more or less as an example of how Americans started out and what they should go back to—to sanity and soundness and away from this jumpiness. It's hard to write humor in the mental weather we've had, and that's likely to take you into reminiscence. Your heart isn't in it to write anything funny. In the years 1950 to 1953 I did very few things, nor did they appear in *The New Yorker*. Now, actually, I think the situation is beginning to change for the better.

INTERVIEWERS: No matter what the "mental climate," though, you would continue writing?

THURBER: Well, the characteristic fear of the American writer is not so much that as it is the process of aging. The writer looks in the mirror and examines his hair and teeth to see if they're still with him. "Oh my God," he says, "I wonder how my writing is. I bet I can't write today." The only time I met Faulkner he told me he wanted to live long enough to do three more novels. He was fifty-three then, and I think he *has* done them. Then Hemingway says, you know, that he doesn't expect to be alive after sixty. But he doesn't look forward *not* to being. When I met Hemingway with John O'Hara in Costello's Bar five or six years ago we sat around and talked about how *old* we were getting. You see it's constantly on the minds of American writers. I've never known a woman who could weep about her age the way the men I know can.

Coupled with this fear of aging is the curious idea that the writer's inventiveness and ability will end in his fifties. And of course it often does. Carl Van Vechten stopped writing. The prolific Joseph Hergesheimer suddenly couldn't write any more. Over here in Europe that's never been the case—Hardy, for instance, who started late and kept going. Of course Keats had good reason to write, "When I have fears that I may cease to be Before my pen has glean'd my teeming brain." That's the great classic statement. But in America the writer is more likely to fear that his brain may cease to teem. I once did a drawing of a man at his typewriter, you see, and all this crumpled paper is on the floor, and he's staring down in discouragement. "What's the matter," his wife is saying, "has your pen gleaned your teeming brain?"

INTERVIEWERS: In your case there wouldn't be much chance of this?

THURBER: No. I write basically because it's so much fun—even though I can't see. When I'm not writing, as my wife knows, I'm miserable. I don't have that fear that suddenly it will all stop. I have enough outlined to last me as long as I live.

Incongruity: Romances for Adults

by Richard C. Tobias

In *The White Deer,* a knight-at-arms asks, "When all is dark within the house, who knows the monster from the mouse?" The question is typical: it contains both the incongruity of a knight worrying about a mouse that we expect of a comic writer but also the suggestion of wider meaning we expect from a writer of Romance. Like a Romancer, Thurber tells stories of knights and ladies, wizards and toymakers, and even of poets to make his most complete statement about the function of the imagination. He writes these books for the same reason that Sir Thomas Malory wrote his Romances of the Round Table. In both Thurber and Malory the action takes place on a human scale completely before the reader's eyes and yet the action refers to larger issues and larger scenes than what we actually see. As in Malory's Romances, the reader recognizes the hero's struggle with his enemies as a representative picture of civilization. Malory proposes the idea of *gentilesse* or *courtoisie* which allows his heroes to triumph; Thurber proposes the creative imagination. Both writers dramatize the particular quality they have chosen as the one thing necessary to preserve a dying civilization. The Romance, in both cases, concentrates on its own foreground, giving completely a world in which everything is immediate. In this world of Romance passions are acted out with pure objectivity to show that the comic incongruity of the stories is really a statement of utmost seriousness and importance.

The most obvious similarity between Malory's Romances and Thurber's stories, however, is the violent times in which both writers lived. When he wrote about Arthur and his knights, Malory was in prison, England was being ravaged by the Wars of the Roses, and Europe by the plague. It was a period of discord and suffering. The

"Incongruity: Romances for Adults" by Richard C. Tobias. From *The Art of James Thurber* (Athens, Ohio: Ohio University Press, 1969). Copyright © 1969 by Richard C. Tobias. Reprinted by permission of the Ohio University Press. The selection given here is the first part of Professor Tobias's chapter.

Romance is, in fact, a kind of narrative that men write when they are overwhelmed by a world of brute force. In Malory's time it was gunpower: in Thurber's, nuclear fission. Malory lamented the decline in chivalry: Thurber inhabited a world which has hardly known a meaning for nobility. In the world of these stories beauty and truth might exist just as Malory recreates French Romances where beauty and truth may exist in spite of the brute, naked, and paralyzing forces rampaging within his sight. As Thurber says in the "Foreword" to *The Thirteen Clocks*, "Unless modern Man wanders down these byways occasionally, I do not see how he can hope to preserve his sanity." *Escape* is the word that leaps to the reader's mind, but these stories are not an attempt at a permanent exit, they are a search for respite, a temporary flight from the pest house into courtly landscapes in which one might find balm for one's wounds and the strength and courage to re-enter the world of pain. Although the stories seem to exist in a never-never land, they recreate the pain of society in a pastoral world where the agony can be understood and where a remedy can be discovered and understood.

Thurber differs from Malory in his greater emphasis on comic incongruity. His stories laugh at the contrast between appearance and reality, while Malory was content to paint a gorgeous tapestry. A king who talks like Harold Ross, editor of the *New Yorker,* is funnier than Arthur modeled on Guy of Warwick. Saviors of society are not usually toymakers, villains do not really slay time. Thurber uses comic incongruity both for laughter and as part of his statement. Although we may laugh at a savior who is a toymaker, we also see that it is precisely his ability to make toys that permits him to triumph over the enemy of his society. The villains who slay time are in fact the archetype of a modern tendency that we abhor. Thurber then expands his vision beyond the vision in Malory by merging the methods of comic incongruity with the landscape of Romance.

Thurber published *Many Moons* in 1943. He followed it with *The Great Quillow* in 1944, *The White Deer* in 1945, *The Thirteen Clocks* in 1950, and *The Wonderful O* in 1957. He does not call them romances. He would undoubtedly be offended by an attempt to name them something fancy. They can be read to children, but they use the distant world of Romance and its ideals to comment on the sterile adult world and to show an answer for adults. Although Thurber has known the power of the imagination in all of his sketches in the 1930's, he only now learns how to dramatize a triumphant vision; one of the stories ends with a marriage festival, the classic way for comedies to end. The Romance provides Thurber with another form (like the fable) by means of which he can fulfill the writer's ancient duty of advising man on his true condition. Behind the guise of a fairy tale he can speak of a world of ideals and delight his reader in the process. He puts real toads, as Marianne Moore advises the writer to do, in an imaginary garden.

Since Wordsworth wrote his "Preface" to *Lyrical Ballads,* our writers have looked more at experience than at the heroic ideals animating civilization. The trivia of experience is the modern plague; it does not kill with swift sureness or violent pain, as Malory's plague did, but it does kill with boredom. There is no plague of trivia in the children's stories. The world is distant, charming, and so complete that we bask in full pleasure in it. Thurber has all the delightful paraphernalia of Kings, Royal Astronomers, Dukes, Jesters, Wizards, Magicians, and Beautiful Ladies. He even has Morgan le Fay (Thurber turns the name around to make it Nagrom Yaf), the villainess of Arthurian romances. Clearly the world is displaced from our trauma. The images are the general images of distance: the Princess is fair, red-lipped, and full-figured. The architecture is gothic and labyrinthine. The landscape is formal, and the language is innocent and naive. Whole scenes are repeated like responses to ritualistic question. In moments of high excitement, characters break into rhythmic speech. In the last three books, Thurber closes scenes with couplets as did the Elizabethan playwrights. The foreground is filled and completed by the rich fabric of the artist's invention; we stand in presence chambers, ride through enchanted landscapes, and view complete courts and villages. All is cool, serene, and formed so that the hero may indeed act and know a truer essence than we know in our experience.

But at our backs we always hear—the trauma of our times. The echo is neither loud nor insistent, but gentle and suggestive. The King in *Many Moons* turns to a counselor and snarls incongruously, "Don't tell me everything you've done for me since 1907." The giant ravaging the landscape in *The Great Quillow* is named *Hunder,* suggesting *Hun* and *plunder* and reminding us of the World Wars. King Clode in *The White Deer* behaves like a well-meaning executive of a medium-sized corporation in tax trouble. In *The Thirteen Clocks,* a tag line from Gilbert and Sullivan—"a thing of shreds and patches"—identifies the wandering minstrel. The villains in *The Wonderful O* recall Robert Louis Stevenson villains or a Congressional investigating committee. In these stories the present hovers in our subconscious just as the Earl of Warwick, the Father of Courtesy, hovers behind Malory's King Arthur. In Thurber, how-

ever, the incongruity has a comic function and encourages us to recognize that the echo of the present is constant, that the subject matter is really our subject matter and not the mere story of jesters and
giants. The landscape is, in fact, our landscape of waste and confusion.

Each Eden has a blight. Each story begins with a representation
of a wasted landscape. In *Many Moons* the young Princess is sick;
unless her father can get her the moon, she will die. *The Great
Quillow* has two wastelands: one is potential and physical, represented by a giant's threat to lay waste the village in three weeks; the
other wasteland is represented by the minds of the town council-
men who ineffectually scramble to discover a plan of appeasement.
The White Deer begins with King Clode and two of his sons dis-
consolately enduring existence; for the third time in the century,
they have destroyed all the game in the kingdom. Since they have
no task or function (recall George Smith in *Is Sex Necessary?*), life
is gone from the kingdom. At the end of *The White Deer*, when
Thurber writes his first marriage scene and classic end of comedy,
King Clode stands, somewhat unsteadily but triumphantly, and
shouts: "Surrounded by these dodderers and dolts, I blow my horn
in waste land, so to speak." The wasteland in *The Thirteen Clocks*
takes the form of coldness. The Duke is so cold that he wears gloves
at all times; he refuses to give the hand of the Princess Saralinda in
marriage "since her hand [is] the only warm hand in the castle."
When the Princess enters the room, the Duke holds "up the palms
of his gloves, as if she were a fire at which to warm his hands." In
The Wonderful O the land is laid waste by robbery. The villains
Black and Littlejack not only remove all of the *o* words from the language including *love, hope,* and *valor,* but they ransack villages,
cities and burial sites to find pelf and jewels (not money and gold in
tombs). Thus in each of the five books, infertility is the basic fact
from which the action begins. The infertility presents the coldness,
the inanition, the robbery and plundering so familiar to us. Thurber never insists that this world is our own; as an artist, he presents
a vision, and we recognize it.

The reader's attention in the typical romance focuses completely
on the struggle between good and evil; the hero faces the paralysis of
the wasteland (evil) and finds a way to recreate society. To magnify
the tension between the opponents in Thurber's stories, conventional Men of Power try obvious and practical solutions to relieve
the infertility. A king turns to his advisers; a town council asks its
members to suggest solutions; lawyers are called in. The applica-

tion of power—intellect, economics, laws—fails and actually increases and threatens the world in the tale. As we recognize the wasteland condition, we further recognize the power which ineffectually tries to bring back life and meaning, for the Men of Power are the equivalents in the world of romance for businessmen, scientists, philosophers, and lawyers. Their inevitable failure sends the land deeper into its infertility and prepares us to rejoice more in the hero's final triumph.

Many Moons, the first of these books published, readily shows Thurber's serious purpose by its presentation of these Men of Power. The King calls three advisers to ask them to get the moon, for his daughter will die unless she can have it. Each adviser responds with a long list of services performed, and from the list we discover that the advisers are archetypes or representatives of the modern dilemma. The Lord High Chamberlain announces pontifically to the King that he has

> . . . got ivory, apes and peacocks, rubies, opals, and emeralds, black orchids, pink elephants and blue poodles, gold bugs, scarabs, and flies in amber, hummingbirds' tongues, angels' feathers, and unicorns' horns, giants, midgets, and mermaids, frankincense, ambergris, and myrrh, troubadors, minstrels and dancing women.

The Lord High Chamberlain has, in short, brought all the joys and wealth of the world to the King; in the world of romance, he represents the prodigious success of commerce and distribution in ministering to the King. Thurber's energetic catalogue makes attractive what the businessman has brought. We are allowed no superficial judgment which condemns businessmen, for what the Chamberlain offers is worthy and admirable. Unfortunately the businessman cannot help at the critical moment in the Kings's rule: he cannot get the moon for the Princess Lenore.

The King next summons his Royal Wizard to get the moon to save the life of the dying Princess. He too has a long list of wonders wrought:

> I have squeezed blood out of turnips for you, and turnips out of blood. I have produced rabbits out of silk hats, and silk hats out of rabbits. I have conjured up flowers, tambourines, and doves. I have brought you divining rods, magic wands, and crystal spheres in which to behold the future. I have compounded philters, unguents, and potions, to cure heartbreak, surfeit, and ringing of the ears. I have made you my own special mixture of wolfbane, nightshade, and eagle's tears, to ward off witches, demons, and things that go bump in the night. I have given you seven league

> boots, the golden touch, and a cloak of invisibility . . . horns from
> elfland, sand from the Sandman, and gold from the rainbow.

Again we are dazzled by the adviser's offerings. The catalogue now,
however, contains sheer wizardry and marvel. His list stands for the
wealth that the technician and the scientist bring to us. But while
his list too is convincing and marvelous, the Royal Wizard cannot
bring life back into the kingdom by granting the wish of the lan-
guishing Princess for the moon. The Wizard's failure is the failure
of technical society to ease human need (although it has done much
for human want); he has much to offer but little to offer in the present human case.

In despair, the King turns to a third hired assistant, the Royal
Mathematician. Again the counselor repeats a list of marvels, for
the Mathematician has

> figured out [for the King] the distance between the horns of a
> dilemma, night and day, and A and Z. [He has] computed how far
> is Up, how long it takes to get to Away, and what becomes of
> Gone. [He has] discovered the length of the sea serpent, the price
> of the priceless, and the square of the hippopotamus. [He knows]
> where you are when you are at Sixes and Sevens, how much Is you
> have to have to make Are, and how many birds you can catch
> with the salt of the ocean—187,796,132 if it would interest you to
> know.

While superficially similar to the other lists and similar in that it
too is an attractive series of accomplishments performed, the final
listing has a quality of terror, of search into unknowable unknowns.
The question of how much *Is* it takes to make *Are* calls to our minds
the modern physicists and linguistic philosophers who probe so
deeply into our universe. Since the Royal Mathematician, the abstract philosopher of our world of experience, cannot obtain the
moon any more than the other two, the sterility and threat linger.
All is dark within the house, or the palace in this case, and our desire for a moment of light is intensified. The stage is set for the en-
trance of the hero, the man of imagination.

The other four books show the same unsuccessful effort to vitalize
a wasted land. In *The Great Quillow* the businessmen on the town
council offer ludicrous but common sense plans to drive off the
Giant Hunder. The Tailor suggests putting needles in the suit the
Giant has ordered; the Cobbler wants to put nails in his new boots.
These respected men—who offer important services to their community in their shoes, clothes and food—cannot meet the special

demands of the new threat. In *The White Deer* a bumbling and ineffectual Palace Wizard, a Royal Recorder, a Royal Physician, and
a Royal Astronomer (who looks at the sky through a pink-tinted
telescope) all fail. In *The Thirteen Clocks* "taverners, travelers, tale-
tellers, tosspots, troublemakers and townspeople" offer barroom wit-
ticism to counter the fearful threat. In *The Wonderful O* the island
lawyer, a man who should aid the community defense against the
robbers and brigands, actually joins forces with the invading host,
Quisling-like, and helps to harry the land. The island-dwellers themselves are so overwhelmed by the threat of Black and Littlejack that
they wait for their own extinction like patient sheep (or the Jews in
Europe) and watch their green and pleasant isle suffer greater and
greater depredation. Thus in the displaced world of romance Thurber makes a significant comment about our civilization. Without the
slightest sense of ridicule and without coruscating irony (without
becoming his enemy and using the enemy tactics), Thurber's world
of romance recreates powerful agents in our society and shows that
they are pitifully unable to serve in crises that go beyond ordinary
mundane problems. The lawyers and businessmen in the world of
romance are perfectly capable of solving questions of law and business, while the scientists are able to explain the phenomenal
world, but all of them are incapable of solving problems of human
meaning. And each failure of these important men—and they must
be highly respected men or else the hero's final victory is hollow or
anti-climactic—prepares us for the hero's triumph.

To communicate the idea of infertility and of the ineffectuality
of the Men of Power, all of the books (except for *Many Moons*)
employ the death of time as a metaphor. Not only is the land
wasted, but because ordinary men cannot do anything to replenish
life, time itself strangely disappears. Thurber makes the connection
between time and events wittily in *The Great Quillow*: the hero,
we are told, looks like a dandelion clock (*clock* is the gardener's
term for the seeds on a dandelion head). The epithet both commu-
nicates the fertility of the toymaker's mind and connects him with
the time ritual in the story. We are told that Quillow's most treas-
ured gift to his community before the giant arrived was his design
of "the twelve scarlet men who emerged from the dial of the town
clock on the strike of every hour." The Giant Hunder, in contrast,
"could wrench a clock from its steeple as easily as a child might remove a peanut from its shell." The story comes to its triumphant
end with a lovely sentence recounting the return of time: "There
the giant was seen no more, and the troubled waters quieted as the

sea resumed its inscrutable cycle of tides under the sun and moon."
In *The White Deer* the sun goes out (and thus time stops) when
King Clode and his sons go hunting for the deer at the beginning
of the book. We are told that one of the good wizards "played with
time" in order to effect the end of the story. The villain-Duke in
The Thirteen Clocks roundly declares his enmity to time:

> . . . I slew [time] . . . and wiped my bloody sword upon its
> beard. . . . If there were light, I'd show you on my sleeves the
> old brown stains of seconds, where they bled and died. I slew
> time in these gloomy halls, and wiped my bloody blade—

The final sentence in the speech trails off, for even the Duke is outside of time. In *The Wonderful O,* Black and Littlejack destroy
time as their first act on the island, and at the end of the book their
defeat is marked by the ringing of a bell which signals the return
of time. Arrested time not only represents the death that ramps
through these kingdoms, but it represents, more necessarily, the loss
of contact with human experience that marks Thurber's villains.
Now is pulsating and alive, but *Then* is cold, controllable, and abstract. The ineffectual solutions offered by the businessmen, the lawyers, the philosophers, and scientists cannot penetrate from the abstract world of *Then* to enter the human world of *Now* where the
crisis of each story takes place and where time exists. The simple,
but arresting, device distinguishes between knowledge or intellect
(the abstract and cold) and intelligence or imagination (creative,
warm, and effective). Intellect functions in the material world; intelligence moves the world of human meaning.

With the land at waste, with the counselors and wizards impo-
tent, and with the clocks stopped, the world of Thurber's five small
books is ready for the true hero who will bring life and time back
into existence. Each hero is a poet, a maker. He has the power to
penetrate through the phenomena of experience to grasp human
meaning. His power of creation is quite visible. The King in *Many
Moons* summons his Royal Jester: the King needs him only to sing
a sad song to ease despair, but providentially the Jester twice finds
a way to act and bring the dying princess to life. Quillow, the toymaker, constructs "hearts of gold for the girls of the town and hearts
of oak for the boys." The third son of King Clode softly strums a
lute and composes verses. The Prince in *The Thirteen Clocks* is a
wandering minstrel. *The Wonderful O* has a poet as its hero. Desig-
nating them as poets and makers, however, is not all that Thurber
does to dramatize the idea of the creative intelligence.

In every book, the hero begins at a lowly station and is treated with contempt. He is an alien, an outsider, whom no one wants. As Malory's Gareth is a bow ready to release its arrow, so the sad treatment of Thurber's heroes sets them on edge to spring at the critical moment. The King in *Many Moons*, for example, looks upon the Jester as a mere device, an agent to take his mind off the coming death of his child. The town council considers Quillow's work as a toymaker "a rather pretty waste of time." His name suggests that he is a hollow reed or quill which the Council blows around for amusement, winding him up as if he were a toy and refusing to admit him to the council. He is present at their meetings only to provide frivolous amusement. Prince Jorn is more fully a male Cinderella. He is the third son who does not like to hunt as his father and brothers do; he speaks truth when pleasant lies would be more convenient. His father contemptuously bets that his two older brothers will easily accomplish the perilous task set for them. The Minstrel Prince in *The Thirteen Clocks* is jovially mocked in the title Prince of Rags. When the *o* is taken from the poet in *The Wonderful O*, he becomes equal to his dog, for then they are both merely pets. The important men in each society treat the poet-heroes contemptuously.

Lowly as each hero is, he has the power to discover the categories of human meaning. He alone acts to bring life and time back into the wasteland, and since he acts after the conventional men of power have failed, his triumph indeed dazzles the reader. Thus the Jester in *Many Moons*, noting that the Chamberlain, Wizard, and Mathematician all describe the moon differently, asks the Princess what the moon is and how large it is. The Princess says that it is no larger than her thumbnail; it is no higher than the tree outside her window; and it is made of gold. The Jester promises to climb the tree that very evening and bring it to her; in fact, he goes to the Goldsmith and has him make a golden moon according to the Jester's instructions.

> The Court Jester took the moon to the Princess Lenore, and she was overjoyed. The next day she was well again and could get up and go out in the gardens to play.

The Jester's pattern of creative intelligence saves each wasteland. Quillow stages a campaign of psychological warfare and convinces the Giant that he has some frightful disease which can only be cured by plunging himself into the sea. Although King Clode and his two eldest sons see "the false flux of fact and form" in their pursuit of the White Deer, Prince Jorn penetrates to what is true in the character of the deer magically transformed into a Princess who has "a memory of fields and meadows, and a memory of nothing more." The hero of *The Thirteen Clocks* needs the full time help of a supernatural agent called the Golux; the Golux, however, clearly represents the power of the imagination. *The Wonderful O* is the most explicit of the five stories; Andreus, the poet, invokes the power of men in fairy tale and legend to defeat Black and Little-jack. In every case, the creative imagination, the poet's power, discovers the secret of fertility to bring life and time back into the dead kingdom.

Thus Thurber dramatizes that high idea of the imagination which enables the poet to "build that dome in air," as Coleridge said, to give life its rich significance and meaning. Meaning, the stories say, does not exist in the world of phenomena; meaning is imposed by the mind, and the mind of the poet—the maker—discovers the meaning for the human heart. Thurber refines and dramatizes the quality of creative intelligence in these books just as Malory's heroes dramatize *courtoisie* and *gentilesse*. Thurber's quality is defined by the foils that he sets beside his heroes so that in contrast to the foil, the true imagination of the hero forces itself into the reader's mind. In *The White Deer* two separate kinds of wizards affect the action: the King's ineffectual palace wizards and the very successful wood wizards who are allied to Prince Jorn, the hero. The palace wizards have been trained in the abstract laws of their science; the wood wizards have acquired a further measure of understanding which we would call the genius of the creative imagination. King Clode diagnoses the failure of the palace wizards:

> Average wood wizards know more in one day than this buffoon [his own palace wizard] learns in ten years, spite of the fact he attended one of the most expensive schools for sorcerers in the world. Bah! can't teach a man to ride a horse or cast a spell. Comes naturally or it doesn't come at all.

The wood wizards, in contrast, have the instinctive sense of identification and creation; this sense comes as the leaves of the tree. Prince Jorn shares this ability, for when he sees the White Deer who is transformed into a Princess, he is not impelled by any irritable reaching after fact or reason as are the palace wizards. He simply loves her. The same naturalness and directness enables the Princess Saralinda to start the thirteen clocks; although "Tinkers and tinkerers and a few wizards who happened by tried to start the clocks with tools or magic words, or by shaking them and cursing," the Princess starts them by *not* touching them. We might compare the quality of the wood wizards and Thurber's heroes with *instinct* in animals, but instinct suggests a mindless quality. It is mindless if we mean by mind the operation of inductive and deductive logic. The quality goes beyond logic to that intuitive, non-discursive grasp of categories of meaning.

If I suggest that these stories should be read as allegories, I have created a wrong impression. They are stories which follow a pattern of meaning: the human imagination is alone capable of comprehending and solving the human situation. The vision may not satisfy all: T. S. Eliot's Anglo-Catholic tradition, absurdists facing absurdity, social causes like Marxism, Liberalism, or Conservatism offer quite different ways of seeing the human experience. The important thing about Thurber is that he can show us the power of the artist and the power of the practical man of affairs without denigrating practical men or traditionalists or Marxists. Inside his faith in the creative imagination, his art finds a way to allow his men and women to act. And thus once more he creates, by his vision, a dome or a mountain from which to view the plain of ordinary experience. An artist can do little more.

The *Male Animal* and the Political Animal

by *Robert E. Morsberger*

Ever since its first run, *The Male Animal* has been popular with college and community theaters. There is opportunity for much amusing stage business; there are a number of good roles for talented performers; and, with skillful direction and cast, it makes a highly successful production. Ohio State presented it in arena style for two weeks in July, 1950. Then in 1952, it was revived in New York at the City Center, with Elliott Nugent again playing the lead, supported by Martha Scott and Robert Preston as Ellen Turner and Joe Ferguson, respectively. Though scheduled for only a two-week run, it had such a favorable reception that it was moved on May 15 to the Music Box for a prolonged showing. In fact the revival played for more performances than the first production, running for 301 performances to the original 244.

The success of this revival has a particular interest, for it was at this time that the House Committee on Un-American Activities was probing into presumed Communist activities on campuses and creating a Red scare similar to that in the play. Most ironically, Thurber's own Ohio State began to suppress academic freedom. Thurber described this situation regretfully in *The Thurber Album*, reporting that, in the fall of 1951, the university's trustees, consisting largely of "aggressively patriotic gentlemen always ready and eager to save America from the perils of academic freedom . . . decided that nobody could speak on campus until he had been intellectually seized and searched to see if his political opinions contained anything that might corrupt the minds of the students, such as Communism, or anything else modern or liberal or radical enough to warrant suspicion." This situation is essentially what happened

"*The Male Animal* and the Political Animal." From Robert E. Morsberger, *James Thurber* (New York: Twayne Publishers, Inc., 1964), pp. 140–48. Copyright © 1964 by Twayne Publishers, Inc. Reprinted by permission of the author and Twayne Publishers, Inc. The selection reprinted here is the last portion of Professor Morsberger's chapter.

twelve years earlier in *The Male Animal.* Furthermore, "While the trustees were qualifying freedom of speech at the university, they decided it was a matter of good old plain common sense, or good old-fashioned Americanism, to qualify freedom of research too." In reaction, scholars boycotted Ohio State, and protests poured in from all quarters, forcing the trustees and administration to loosen their restrictions.

Thurber observed that for years before this, legislative interference at Ohio State had been a thorn in the side of academic freedom. But he maintained that, "a communist speaker could not possibly sway an Ohio State audience and that in refusing to let communists talk, the university deprives itself of a wonderful chance to heckle and confound such speakers. If we cannot be strong enough Americans to withstand such arguments, if we are in such danger of being politically debauched, then all we have in the Western conference is the greatest football area in the world. . . .[1] Accordingly, Thurber refused an honorary degree from Ohio State University in protest against the 1951 gag rule.

If *The Male Animal* was daringly outspoken in 1940, it was doubly so in 1952 when the late Senator McCarthy and his associates were at the height of their power. The very real danger to academic freedom no doubt gave the revival of the play an immediacy that contributed to its success, and its reception shows that a large segment of the theater-going public endorsed Thurber's and Nugent's indictment of inquisitorial practices. But inquisitors are a touchy lot, and they reply to criticism by attempting to smear the character of their critics and to label them as agents of the devil's party. When the Laguna Beach Playhouse in California performed *The Male Animal* in 1952, the South Coast *News* denounced it with the headline, "Americans attacked at Playhouse!" and its anonymous drama critic went on to accuse the play of ridiculing sincere Americanism like Ed Keller's. "One gets the impression," he wrote, "of being told that, as a group, college trustees, administrators, and even realistic faculty wives are lacking in ideals, toady to the ogre of big business, and are unappreciative of the teaching profession." Like Ed Keller, this critic also said that the play has no business to include a speech of Vanzetti's.[2]

Like Cyrano, Thurber replied sarcastically that the critic was not adequate in his insults; he forgot to add Thurber's other subver-

[1] James E. Pollard, "James Thurber," in *Ohio Authors and Their Books 1796–1950,* ed. William Coyle (Cleveland and New York, 1962), p. 635.
[2] *Theatre Arts,* XXVIII (October, 1954), 15.

sions, such as "my effort to prevent the building of college football stadia, my special pleading on behalf of extramarital relations, and my attack on the competence of Republican presidents, which shows up in the line, 'Hoover can't write as well as Vanzetti.' " Apparently, even before this attack, Thurber had been accused of un-Americanism. In 1948, he referred ironically to *The Male Animal* as "a subversive play" of 1940. "But," he added sarcastically, "I have promised to submit any plays I may write in the future to either Congressman Thomas or Mrs. Lela Rogers, the eminent authorities on the Drama . . ." "People ask why there isn't a comedy like *The Male Animal* anymore—something that's free and exuberant," said Thurber in 1952. "It isn't possible to write a comedy like that anymore because we're living in the most frightened century in the world." [3] He claimed that McCarthy's Congressional probes—"more of a political device than a patriotic endeavor"—made the Broadway theater "moribund and demoralized"; and he recalled that, during the 1952 revival of his play, the audience was tense rather than relaxed.

Certainly it is apparent to any clear-minded reader that the play does not have any leanings towards communism. It does not champion Communist professors; its point is that the discharged faculty members have been accused unjustly. Even Michael Barnes, the radical student who started the furor, is not a Communist but "an unconfused liberal." Turner himself is not actively interested in politics until they are thrust upon him. As one critic commented, "Professor Turner really hasn't any potential pinkness. He just happens to think that a man called Vanzetti once wrote a very well expressed letter, and happened to say so much to a boyfriend of his sister-in-law's who exploited it in a student editorial." Thurber, too, was no insurrectionist; he wrote in 1960 that "It is comforting, in a vaguely uneasy way, to realize that American students do not engage in political demonstrations, but reserve their passions for panty raids, jazz festivals, and the hanging of football coaches in effigy."

In fact, Thurber always showed hostility toward communism, even in the 1930's, when it was fashionable for some writers and intellectuals to dabble in it. Though the Red Decade is no doubt a misleading label for that period, Marxist criticism was militant and influential, and proletarian literature was prominent. Writers suspicious of communism were attacked as intolerant and accused

---

[3] Harvey Breit, *The Writer Observed* (Cleveland and New York, 1956), p. 256.

of kicking the underdog. In the midst of the Depression, it required particularly acute thinkers to perceive—through all the defiant slogans—that though capitalism was indeed sick and in need of surgery, the Communist alternative might prove fatal. When such able writers as Clifford Odets, John Dos Passos, Ernest Hemingway, Malcolm Cowley, and Granville Hicks were not yet disenchanted with the Soviet "experiment," liberal but unsympathetic critics like Thurber and E. E. Cummings, both irreverent humorists and ardent advocates of individual liberty against any dogmatic restraints, were viewed by the left with resentment and dismay. Traditionalists like Willa Cather and Thornton Wilder were condemned as cowards. The *New Yorker* writers who stayed aloof from didactic proletarian prose were dismissed by Mike Gold as a bunch of "college punks."

Incensed, Thurber wrote Malcolm Cowley of *The New Republic* a fifteen-page letter assailing literary communism. Cowley replied by inviting Thurber to review Granville Hicks's edition of *Proletarian Literature in the United States* (1936). In an unbiased critique, based on literary merit, Thurber praised some selections but complained that too many degenerated into invective and irrelevant insult against "bourgeois" writers. He was particularly irritated by Joseph Freeman's "sweeping insinuation" that the middle class consisted of lechers and Narcissists and that love is confined to the proletariat. On artistic grounds, he objected not to the subject matter but to the too-often slipshod prose: "I grant the importance of the scenes on which all these stories are based, but they cannot have reality, they cannot be literature, if they are slovenly done. . . . Art does not rush to the barricades." Thurber advised the proletarian authors to study the work of such *New Yorker* writers as Robert Coates and St. Clair McKelway, whose "writing is hard, painstaking and long." And a final and fatal defect was the anthology's total lack of humor. "The nature of humor is anti-communistic just as the nature of Communism is anti-humor," wrote Thurber seventeen years later during the Red scare.

Objecting to the dogmatism of Marxist critics, Thurber devoted two essays to them *Let Your Mind Alone* (1937), ridiculing their dialectic ("the process of discriminating one's own truth from another person's error") and factionalism ("that process of disputation by means of which the main point of issue is lost sight of"). A fastidious stylist, he disliked their addiction to jargon and the pretentious and calculated quality of their elaborate autobiographical correspondence. Since it seemed that the main purpose of leftist literary meetings was to unmask everybody else's ideology,

Marxist criticism struck Thurber as being very similar to psycho-analysis: "Ideology-unmasking is a great deal like dream interpretation and leads to just as many mystic results."

Art cannot be regimented, and Thurber concluded that he was "opposed to every restriction, mould, pattern, and commandment for literature that is set up by the Marxist literary critics." Three years earlier, in "Notes for a Proletarian Novel," he had ridiculed Granville Hicks for believing "that Emily Dickinson failed miserably in her lyrics about bees because she didn't give any serious attention to the problem of the workers." Thus he challenged Malcolm Cowley, "If these men, who write such attacks, should ever get in control, do you think there wouldn't be a commissar of literature who would be appointed and commissioned to stop it, who would set us at work writing either poems in praise of the American Lenin or getting up time tables for work trains? If you do, you're missing a low, faint, distant rumbling." [4] Actually, Thurber didn't think there was any chance of such a revolution. "I believe the only menace is the growing menace of fascism," he wrote to Cowley. "I also firmly believe that it is the clumsy and whining and arrogant attitude of the proletarian writers which is making the menace bigger every day." [5]

In his zeal to oppose fascism, Thurber was among four hundred signers of the Open Letter denouncing—just before the Nazi-Soviet pact—"the fantastic falsehood that the USSR and the totalitarian states are basically alike" and criticizing the Committee for Cultural Freedom that had included the USSR among totalitarian states. But Eugene Lyons, author of *The Red Decade*, concedes that the signers, "prominent people from all sections of the country," wanted to attack Nazism, not defend the Soviets, and that these mostly reputable citizens were duped by the double talk of the form letter, which he calls "a masterpiece of political jugglery." [6]

Ed Keller's ghost was not laid to rest, for in the post World War II years, Thurber was alarmed by the internal peril to the American scene from the investigations and inquisitorial techniques practiced by some government committees and self-righteous civic groups of the extreme right, whose irresponsible accusations of disloyalty, he felt, created an era of fear and uncertainty. He lamented the de-

4 Malcolm Cowley, "A Job to Do," in "Salute to Thurber," *The Saturday Review*, XLIV (November 25, 1961), 15.

5 *Ibid.*

6 Eugene Lyons, *The Red Decade, The Stalinist Penetration of America* (Indianapolis and New York, 1941), pp. 347, 350–51.

cline of political satire at this time, when all writers were suspect. Thurber said sarcastically that he himself might appear guilty to the three-man inquisitions run by the State Department in 1947: "I believed then, and still do, that generals of the Southern Confederacy were, in the main, superior to generals of the Northern armies; I suspected there were flaws in the American political system; I doubted the virgin birth of United States senators; I thought that German cameras and English bicycles were better than ours; and I denied the existence of actual proof that God was exclusively a citizen of the United States."

It appears that Thurber and other perfectly loyal writers had some reason for apprehension; for Malcolm Cowley, in his study of the current literary situation, revealed that in practice—though not in theory—the restrictions on travel abroad were more heavily imposed on the writing profession than on any other; the investigators seemed to have an instinctive hostility to writers, who might criticize the political scene. "As for positions with the government," Cowley observed, "very few writers applied for them after 1950, word having gotten around that anyone who had published a book was likely to get into trouble with Congress. Roy M. Cohn, chief counsel for Senator McCarthy's subcommittee, might have been speaking for many Congressmen when he was asked about the choice of speakers for a television program and said, 'Any author is out.'" [7] Thurber protested our taking the passport away from Arthur Miller, to whom a Congressman had asked, "Do you really believe that the artist is a special person?" Thurber replied in the New York *Times*: "A nation in which a Congressman can seriously ask: 'Do you think the artist is a special person?' is a nation living in cultural jeopardy." Coming to his colleagues' defense, Thurber stated that most writers he knew always hated communism, "but they have the curiosity of male spaniel puppies or female spotted deer. They get into things, but this can be defended on the sound ground that nothing can be intelligently accepted or rejected unless it has been examined and understood." "If we don't stop suspecting all writers," he said in 1952, "it will be a severe blow to our culture. I think all writers, even the innocent ones, are scared. There's guilt by association, guilt by excoriation, there's guilt by everything the politicians invent." [8]

There was, even for the acquitted, what Thurber called guilt by exoneration—a stigma attached to one for having been suspect at

[7] Malcolm Cowley, *The Literary Situation* (New York, 1954), pp. 221–22.
[8] Breit, *loc. cit.*

all. As early as 1948, Thurber complained of the atmosphere engendered by such finger-pointing and remarked that, "In the present Era of Suspicion, it is a wise citizen who disproves any dark rumors and reports of his secret thoughts and activities before they can be twisted into charges of disloyalty by the alert and skillful minds now dedicated to that high-minded and patriotic practice." He feared that such heresy-hunting repressed satire or any criticism of the political scene. If the expression of humor was stifled, he felt that the danger was as great of our being destroyed from within as from without because we were fighting the enemy with its own weapons. "As a matter of fact," he wrote in his reply to the Ohioana award, "comedy, in all its forms, including the rusty art of political satire, is used to surviving eras of stress and strain, even of fear and trembling, but it sickens in the weather of intimidation and suppression, and such a sickness could infect a whole nation. The only rules comedy should tolerate are those of taste and the only limitations those of libel."

VI The Necessity of Satire

Thurber liked to think of himself as a sharp-penned and sometimes savage satirist rather than as the harmless humorist some careless readers took him to be. On television ("Small World," March 22, 1959), he said that he preferred Mencken to Will Rogers for American political satire, since Rogers never said anything dangerous or daring. This statement does not mean that Thurber was indiscriminately iconoclastic; for he would doubtless have agreed with Swift that, "although some Things are too serious, solemn, or sacred to be turned into Ridicule, yet the Abuses of them are certainly not. . . ." Insofar as he distinguishes truth from hypocrisy, cant, and fraud, the satirist is a public servant. Believing that whatever is genuine can endure the test of laughter, Thurber insisted that "Our comedy should deal, in its own immemorial manner, with the American scene and the American people, without fear or favor, without guilt or grovelling."

Ordinarily apolitical in his work, Thurber wrote most of his political satire after the advent of McCarthy, who aroused rather than intimidated him, and whom he compared to an enormous caterpillar eating the vegetation of the Republic. In 1958, he told Henry Brandon that "The six or eight years that went by—those terrible years—when all the American Congress seemed to do was to investigate writers, artists and painters—to me were the dreadful years. All this time Russia was getting ahead of us, all this time we were fighting a new cold civil war—suspecting neighbors, suspecting the very nature of writing, of academic intellectualism, anything—that was a very bad moment in our history—perhaps the darkest we've ever had. But I think we're coming out of that." [9]

During the height of heresy-hunting, even Thurber needed some mental relief; and he confessed that he wrote *The Thurber Album* partly to return to the placid years of his parents' generation—"the age of innocence, when trust flowered as readily as suspicion does today. . . ." Thus, "The *Album* was a kind of escape—going back to the Middle West of the last century and the beginning of this, when there wasn't this fear and hysteria. I wanted to write the story of some solid American characters, more or less as an example of how Americans started out and what they should go back to. To sanity and soundness and away from this jumpiness. It's hard to write humor in the mental weather we've had, and that's likely to take you into reminiscence." [10] Actually, though Thurber stated that, "In 1918, Americans naively feared the enemy more than they feared one another," the Red scare after World War I was in some ways more extreme than McCarthyism; and Attorney-General Palmer was even more high-handed in his suppression of civil liberties.

Ironically, many of the witch-hunters themselves also want to return to the simpler past, when "solid American characters" were supposedly more common. Hysterical reactionaries, labeling the entire contemporary scene as subversive, frequently clamor for the virtues of the Old Frontier and its lynch-law justice. Thus William S. Schlamm, writing in the ultra-conservative *Freeman* in 1952, took Thurber to task for not siding with McCarthy and insisted that Robert Ryder and all the characters in *The Thurber Album* would have supported the Wisconsin senator, since the "last refuge of honor and guts and cockeyed friendliness" was on his side.[11] But in the *Album,* Thurber praised as Robert Ryder's greatest paragraph: "A hardened reformer never seems able to make up his mind which is the most beautiful word in the language, 'compulsory' or 'forbidden.' " McCarthy is the perfect example of such a reformer, and it is unlikely that Ryder or any of the other individualists in the *Album* would submit to the bullying of a humorless demagogue.

Schlamm wanted to enlist Thurber as an ally; but some "super-

[9] Henry Brandon, *As We Are* (Garden City, 1961), p. 268.

[10] *Writers at Work*, p. 97.

[11] William S. Schlamm, "The Secret Lives of James Thurber," *Freeman*, II (July 28, 1952), 738.

patriots," apparently using the logic that, since he opposed witch-hunting, he must be a witch, labeled him as subversive. Thurber said that he was always, in fact, "a vehement anti-communist, a fact that could be proved in a few hours of research, but I have no doubts that, like almost all writers, I will one day be named as a Red." [12] Since he dared write *The Male Animal* and was one of the bitterest critics of Senator McCarthy and the more recent rabble rousers of the radical right, we find that the pamphlet, "Red Stars—No. 3," issued in 1960 by the Cinema Educational Guild, Inc., includes Thurber among the "best known of the REDS and FELLOW-TRAVELERS who made our SCREEN Communism's most effective 'Pied Piper,'" with "films that sanctify MARXISM—ONE-WORLDISM—DESEGREGATION." This hysterical document accuses a long list of artists of "brainwashing and poisoning your children right under your very eyes" and urges each individual to boycott their work and to drive them from the theater. Along with a few acknowledged Communists, the list includes such "subversive" figures as Thurber, Danny Kaye, Sir Douglas Fairbanks, Jr., Bennett Cerf, Edward R. Murrow, Chet Huntley, Gypsy Rose Lee, Groucho Marx, Burgess Meredith, Leonard Bernstein, Aaron Copland, Agnes DeMille, Sidney Poitier, Oscar Hammerstein II, Moss Hart, George S. Kaufman, Archibald MacLeish, Dorothy Parker, and dozens of other perfectly innocent people. The pamphlet provides no evidence (because there is none) but relies upon mere slander and libel.

But, wrote Thurber, "Guilt is not a matter of guesswork or conjecture, but of proof." Thus from the fable of "The Very Proper Gander" (1940) to that of "The Peacelike Mongoose" (1956), he attacked those who would, on the basis of hearsay or other insufficient evidence, denounce their neighbors as traitors, with the result that, "if the enemy doesn't get you your own folks may." Lamenting the decline of "the old abandoned American assumption of innocence" until one is proven guilty, Thurber invented several holidays to remedy the situation. These include Fact Day, when "only the proved is tolerated"; Liability Day, when senators and congressmen "would be deprived of immunity and could be sued for libellous remarks"; and (to balance the scales) Immunity Day, when anyone could freely criticize anybody. "Many persons, in our era of fear and hysteria," he wrote in 1955, "are afraid to say what they think about public figures and national affairs, and have become neurotic victims of ingrown reticence, no longer able to tell

12 Pollard, p. 635.

discretion from timidity, or conviction from guilt." Even the comic strips were under attack: some papers censored *Pogo*, and Al Capp was pressured to remove the Schmoo from *Li'l Abner* and to tone down the strip generally because it seemed to some "super-patriots" to be suspect in its satire of military and business interests. Despite Mike Gold's leftist attack upon it, *The New Yorker* was now denounced as "Red from top to bottom," and was sufficiently intimidated in 1956 that it refused to print some of Thurber's political fables—the very ones that won him the American Library Association's Liberty and Justice Award.

"Humor should never take the form of penance or of penitence," Thurber insisted, for a free society decays in an atmosphere of humorlessly grim self-righteousness that proscribes healthy self-criticism. The methods of Ed Keller and McCarthy are too similar to those of the Soviets, and it is impossible to retain freedom by employing the tactics of its enemies. "Well, there isn't a trace of humor in communism, is there? I think any political system that vehemently attacks humor reveals a great weakness," Thurber told Harvey Breit.[13] In 1960, he charged that comedy had been beaten by both the intellectual left and the political right. "Humor, as Lord Boothby has said, is the only solvent of terror and tension, and terror and tension are among the chief ideological weapons of Communism." Besides, tyrants and bigots have always feared laughter because it shows them up "in a clear and honest light and drives away the big distorted shadows in which they love to lurk." Hence Thurber opposed demagogues of any sort, whether of the extreme right or left. Enemies to laughter, both would strangle freedom of expression; and it was for this freedom rather than for any specific political program that Thurber fought. In *The Male Animal*, Keller says that he would not allow the Vanzetti letter to be read under any circumstances. "I wouldn't care if that letter were by Alexander Hamilton." "Neither would I," replies Turner; "the principle is exactly the same."

13 Breit, p. 257.

Lions and Lemmings, Toads and Tigers

by Malcolm Cowley

Aesop's animals are Greek citizens, and those of La Fontaine are French peasants or noblemen, with the lion as *Le Grand Monarque*. It is only proper that Thurber's animals should be the mirrors of a new society which seems to consist of college-bred Americans with more bright gadgets than they need and with more neuroses than they can afford.

I suspect that most of them were born in Columbus, Ohio, like the author, and that they have followed him into the Connecticut jungle where they feel at home: lions and lemmings, toads and tigers, wolves and gaudy young wolfesses, all of them busy at their avocations of driving too fast, drinking too much if they are males, worrying about the children if they are mothers, and getting into family arguments. These are usually won by the females, who have the inborn advantage of knowing exactly what they want, which is everything.

In the first of the new fables, two almost shapeless creatures crawl out of the sea at the almost beginning of time. The male feels uneasy in the new environment and globs back into the water (the verb "to glob" is one of Thurber's many inventions), but the female goes flobbering almost imperceptibly toward the scrubby brown growth beyond the sand, while dreaming of things that will later become rose-point lace, taffeta, and jewelry. A couple of eons later, the male feels lonely and comes flobbering after her. And the moral of the story? "Let us ponder this basic fact about the human: Ahead of every man, not behind him, is a woman."

Often in the fables we find the sexes joined in single or wedded combat. A grizzly bear comes home after a month-long bender after a Christmas party to find that his wife has filled the house with lamps that emit an odor of pine cones, chairs that bounce him up and down, cigarette boxes that can't be opened, and supersafety matches that won't light. He smashes the furniture, throws the gadgets out of the window, and goes roaring away with the most attractive of the unmarried female bears, one named Honey. Moral: "Nowadays most men lead lives of noisy desperation." In another fable Proudfoot the tiger is consistently rude to his wife, who rebels one night. Next morning the cubs, male and female, tumble eagerly downstairs while calling to their mother, "What can we do?" She tells them, "You can go in the parlor and play with your father. He's the tiger rug just in front of the fireplace." Moral: "Never be mean to a tiger's wife, especially if you're the tiger."

Though he reports a number of these bloody skirmishes, there is a softer note in many of Thurber's latest communiqués about the war between men and women. He is no longer the stern male patriot that he was in the days when he drew a woman's face on the dragon waiting to devour a timid St. George. As a good moralist, he warns each woman not to be a bragdowdy (in Thurber's definition, a woman who admits, often proudly, that she has let herself go—a frumpess); a hugmoppet (an overaffectionate old woman, a bunny-talker); a starefrock (a woman who stares another woman up and down—hence, a rude female, a hobbledehoyden); or an interfering busybody. "Thou shalt not convert thy neighbor's wife," he tells her, "nor yet louse up thy neighbor's life."

But he also warns each man—here or in other recent work—not to be a snatchkiss (Thurber's word for a kitchen lover); a smug-bottle (a man, usually American, who boasts of his knowledge of wines—a fussgrape); or a growp (like Proudfoot the tiger, who kept snarling "Growp," by which he actually meant, "I hope the cubs grow up to be xylophone players or major generals").

Perhaps Thurber thinks of himself as having risen above the hurly-burly *au dessus de la mêlée*.

The Age of Gudda

At sixty-one, almost sixty-two, he is becoming more inventive in his language but more traditional in his wisdom. The fables find new ways of telling us that all is vanity, that beauty is no more fleeting than ugliness, and that misery loves company but can't always find it. Some of the morals are: "The noblest study of man-kind is Man, says Man"; "Where most of us end up there is no knowing, but the hellbent get where they are going"; "It is wiser to be hendubious than cocksure"; "This is the posture of fortune's slave: one foot in the gravy, one foot in the grave"; "You can't very well be the king of beasts if there aren't any"—this for a story of total war in the jungle; and "A word to the wise is not sufficient if it doesn't make any sense," for a fable about the chaos of the English language.

This last has become what is probably his favorite subject of warning. The animals in his fables, like the persons in his stories are always misunderstanding one another and jumping to fatal conclusions. "Get it right," he tells them, "or leave it alone. The conclusion you jump to may be your own." He also says, "We live, man and worm, in a time when almost everything can mean almost anything, for this is the age of gobbledygook, double talk, and gudda." Consulting *The Thurber Album,* one learns that gudda, a language spoken in the environs of Columbus, Ohio, is so named for the word that most frequently pops up in it. The word is a verb of possession ("I gudda horse"), of necessity ("I gudda get a horse"), and of futurity ("I'm gudda get a horse tmawra"). Thurber still talks like a man from Columbus—that is, fast and through his nose—but he never uses gudda except when he is doing impersonations. His effort through most of a long career has been to write lucid, correct, and expensively simple English.

I would hesitate to say that his prose is the best now being written in this country. Other things being equal, the best prose would be that which was most effective in presenting the boldest subjects. Except in his fables, where he can touch them lightly, Thurber has always avoided bold subjects like war and revolution, love and death; he prefers to write about the domestic confusions of people whose sedentary lives are not too different from his own. It isn't a very complicated society that he presents, or one with a rich fabric of inherited values, or one in which men and women are destroyed by their splendid passions. His most ambitious hero is Walter Mitty, who has his visions of glory while buying puppy biscuits. His tragic lover (in "The Evening's at Seven") goes back to a *table d'hôte* dinner at his hotel and, in token of a shattered life, orders consommé instead of clam chowder.

Comedy is his chosen field, and his range of effects is deliberately limited, but within that range there is nobody who writes better than Thurber, that is, more clearly and flexibly, with a deeper feeling for the genius of the language and the value of words.

He tries never to intone or be solemn. "Humor," he once wrote in a letter to me, "cannot afford the ornaments and indulgences of fine writing, the extravagance of consciousness-streaming, or lower-case unpunctuation meanderings. There is a sound saying in the theater: 'You can't play comedy in the dark.' I saw Jed Harris and Billy Rose trying to disprove this one night in Philadelphia twenty-five years ago when they put on an eight-minute Don Marquis skit in absolute darkness: the sounds of voices, glasses, and the cash register of an old-time beer saloon. People fell asleep, or began coughing, or count-ing their change, or whispering to their neighbors, or reading their programs with pencil flashlights. Comedy has to be done *en clair*. You can't blunt the edge of wit or the point of satire with obscur-ity."

In his effort to be absolutely clear, he pays so much attention to the meaning and color of words that he speaks of them almost as if they had personalities to be cultivated or avoided. "What could be worse than 'eroticize'?" he asked in another letter. "It is one of those great big words, or tortured synonyms, with which psychi-atry has infected the language, so that a page of type sometimes looks like a parade of Jack Johnsons wearing solid gold teeth and green carnations in the lapels of their electric-blue morning suits." He prefers the familiar words that would be used in conversation without a self-conscious pause. His art consists in arranging them so that they give the impression of standing cleanly and separately on the page, each in its place like stones in a well-built wall.

That impression is not an easy one to achieve, and Thurber takes endless pains with his stories. He spent fifty working days on "The Secret Life of Walter Mitty," which is four thousand words long. By contrast he did a whole book of fifty drawings, *The Last Flower*, in two hours of an otherwise idle evening. He has often explained to art critics that he draws for relaxation, as others doodle at the telephone. He never redraws, but he continually rewrites. Last year he told an interviewer that one of his stories—"The Train on Track Six," still unpublished—had been rewritten fifteen times from beginning to end. "There must have been close to 240,000 words in all the manuscripts put together," he said, "and I must have spent two thousand hours working at it. Yet the finished version can't be more than twenty thousand words."

Not with a Bang but with Babble

His gradual loss of eyesight, now almost total, once threatened to put an end to his work. As early as 1941 he found that he could no longer distinguish the keys of a typewriter. When a series of pain-ful operations failed to restore his vision, he took to writing with a black crayon on yellow copy paper. But his one eye kept growing weaker—the other had been lost in a boyhood accident—and his handwriting larger in compensation, until twenty words filled a page and a hundred used up the crayon. Nobody except his wife and his secretary could decipher what he had written.

Then slowly he trained himself to give dictation. It was harder for him than for most writers, because so much of his work depends on his finding exactly the right word and using it in exactly the right place, but at last he found a practical system that he follows most of the time. He spends the morning turning over the text in his mind, moving words around like a woman redecorating the living room, and then in the afternoon he calls in a secretary. The system would be impossible without his remarkable memory. Sometimes he remembers, word for word, three complete versions of the same story.

His loss of vision has had an effect on his style that will be noted by almost every reader of his new fables. All the sound effects have been intensified, as if one sense had developed at the cost of another, and the language is full of onomatopoeia and alliteration. "The caves of ocean bear no gems," one studious lemming reflects as all the others plunge into the water, "but only soggy glub and great gobs of mucky gump." Man tells the dinosaur, in one of the best fables, "You are one of God's moderately amusing early experiments . . . an excellent example of Jehovah's jejune juvenilia." There are puns too, like "Monstrosity is the behemother of extinction," and there are rhymes not only in the morals but scattered through the text, so that whole passages could be printed as verse.

But this preoccupation with words, with their sound, sense, and arrangement into patterns, has affected more than the style of the fables. It is also transforming the imagination of the author, who seems to be presenting us with a completely verbalized universe. The only conceivable end for the inhabitants of such a universe would be mass suicide resulting from complete verbal confusion; and that is exactly how Thurber pictures them as ending, in the fable about lemmings which also ends the collection.

It seems that a single excited lemming started the exodus by crying "Fire!" when he saw the rising sun. Hundreds followed him toward the ocean, then thousands, each shouting a different message of fear or exultation. "It's a pleasure jaunt!" squeaked an elderly female lemming. "A treasure hunt!" echoed a male who had been up all night; "Full many a gem of purest ray serene the dark unfathomed caves of ocean bear." His daughter heard only the last word and shouted, "It's a bear! Go it!" Others among the fleeing thousands shouted "Goats!" and "Ghosts!" until there were almost as many different alarms as there were fugitives. Then they all plunged into the seas, and that was the end of the lemmings.

Symbolically it was also the end of mankind as only Thurber could have imagined it: not with a bang, not with a whimper, but in a universal confusion of voices and meanings.

Thurber's Fifteen-Year Journey

by Gerald Weales

James Thurber's fifteen-year journey from *Fables for Our Time* (1940) to *Further Fables for Our Time* has taken him, as it has taken all of us, through a world war, immediate postwar period of hope for peace that has begun to go a little sour in our mouths, the years of the McCarthy ascendancy when fear and distrust were served up with our breakfast coffee, into the present moment when social conformity has become such a force that even the anti-conformists appear to be conforming. Thurber's own steps through these times have been further darkened by the gradual loss of his sight. The new fables are quite plainly marked with the national and personal uneasiness that these years represent. They are harsher and more bitter than the early fables without succumbing to a facile or fashionable despair; they are richer, wiser, more serious, and, by comparison, the early fables now seem flip and a little smart-alecky.

It is difficult to put a precise finger on the change that has come over the fables, since it is the impact of the new collection as a whole that engenders the sense of sorrowful solidity. A comparison of representative fables, however, may at least suggest what has happened. Compare, for instance, an earlier fable, "The Little Girl and the Wolf" with "The Truth About Toads." Both of these fables hinge on violence and destruction, as do so many of the fables in both collections, but in the tale of the toad there is death with a difference. "The Little Girl and the Wolf" is a variation on the Red Riding Hood story, and ends, "So the little girl took an automatic out of her basket and shot the wolf dead." The moral is, "It is not so easy to fool little girls nowadays as it used to be." The intention is plainly comic; the effect is made by the abruptness of the last line. In "The Truth About Toads" Thurber is much more serious. In

"Thurber's Fifteen-Year Journey" (editor's title). From Gerald Weales, "The World in Thurber's Fables," *The Commonweal*, LV (January 18, 1957). Copyright © 1957 by *The Commonweal*. Reprinted by permission of Commonweal Publishing Co., Inc.

fact, nothing in the new collection has the playfulness of a fable like "The Little Girl and the Wolf." His toad is one of a group of braggart animals having drinks at the Fauna Club. The Toad, who insists that he has a jewel in his head, is the most vociferous of all, and when he drops into a sleep, induced by too many green mint frappés, the other members of the club decide to investigate. "They summoned the Woodpecker from the back room and explained what was up. 'If he hasn't got a hole in his head, I'll make one,' said the Woodpecker." Had the fable ended here its tone would have been much like the earlier one, for the words of the Woodpecker are as sharp and sudden and as callous as the little girl drawing her automatic. But Thurber goes on, echoing the words of the Toad's bragging, "There wasn't anything there, gleaming or lovely or precious." The moral is harsh and a little hurt: "Open most heads and you will find nothing shining, not even a mind."

This new bitterness, which might more accurately be called a new kind of strength or a new order of wisdom or, even, a new depth of beauty, is apparent throughout the *Further Fables.* In the story of the bat who wanted to live among people but who, after having been exposed to a popular evangelist, went resignedly back to his cave, the new element is present not only in the story and its moral, but in Thurber's description of the "best-selling Inspirationalist . . . dragging God down to the people's level." It is there in the last words of his tale of the gloomy bluebird who developed agoraphobia and went to live underground: "the bewildered dog . . . dug him up one day while burying a bone, and then hastily buried him again, without ceremony or sorrow." It pervades "The Clothes Moth and the Luna Moth," which is in many ways the loveliest and saddest of the new fables. It is in the words of the jaguar over the grave of William, the vain cat who lost his memory: "What's the good of putting up a stone reading 'Here lies Nobody from Nowhere'?" It is wisely, if shudderingly, there in the words of the little girl, whose godfather has offered her anything she wants: "I want to break your glasses and spit on your shoes." It is in the credo of the red squirrel in "The Turtle Who Conquered Time": "The truth is not merry and bright. The truth is cold and dark. Let's face it."

The somber streaks that run with the laughter in the new fables are not completely new to Thurber, not a sudden reversal or discovery, not the unveiling of a new man. Thurber said in an interview with Alistair Cooke on *Omnibus* (printed in *The Atlantic,* August, 1956), "It's very hard to divorce humor from other things in life. Humor is the other side of tragedy. Humor is a serious thing." Humor has always been serious for Thurber. Back in 1929, E. B. White wrote a mock serious explanation of Thurber's drawing, which appeared at the end of their *Is Sex Necessary?* Although White's note kids the pretentiousness of critical over-elaboration, just as the book kids the terrible solemnity of all sex books, his remarks cannot escape being touched with truth. "When one studies the drawings," White writes, "it soon becomes apparent that a strong undercurrent of grief runs through them." The music of the line is not quite right, too portentous to be White seriously on Thurber, and yet the words are true. Art critics, particularly in Europe, have accepted this view of Thurber's drawings, although the artist himself insists (in the *Omnibus* appearance; in an interview with George Plimpton and Max Steele in the *Paris Review*, Fall, 1955) that his drawings were (until his failing sight made them impossible) the relaxation from his serious work of writing. Certainly Thurber has given testimony to the dark note that runs through humor, as long ago as the funny and moving "A Note at the End" which brought to a close *My Life and Hard Times* (1933). Stories like "The Secret Life of Walter Mitty" and the more grueling "Whippoorwill," in which he admits an element of anger, a reaction to a series of eye operations that plagued him at the time of writing, had already sounded the frustration and terror that peek occasionally out of the new fables. Enough—too much in fact—has already been written about Thurber and the battle of the sexes, but all that has been written—the elaboration, the interpretation, the psychologizing—has served only to repeat that, like all really good funny men, Thurber is finally deadly serious.

Thurber's relationship to politics has never been an overt one, yet a political climate informs all his later work, either directly or by implication. The early fables contained a few stories—"The Birds and the Foxes" and "The Rabbits Who Caused All the Trouble"—which were direct attacks on the indifference with which the democratic nations faced the spreading power of the Nazis. These old fables sound just as topical today, although at the moment the foxes and the wolves (in the one about the rabbits) will sound more like the Russians than the Germans, for it is any dealers in oppression who mask their ruthlessness in fine phrases that are the target of Thurber's anger. The new collection has the fable of "The Bears and the Monkeys" with its moral, "It is better to have the ring of freedom in your ears than in your nose," to say again what must continually be said about deception and oppression and freedom.

experiments had already begun to sing triumphantly in *The Thirteen Clocks.*

But the strength of *Further Fables* lies in more than a balance of word music against a harsh and sometimes angry view of the world, seen through darkness darkly. It lies in a kind of faith that pervades the whole work, even at its saddest. The opening fable, "The Sea and the Shore," finds some amorphous water creatures crawling toward the undergrowth on land, life in its beginnings; the last fable, "The Shore and the Sea," finds the lemmings, panicked by misunderstanding, in a headlong race to destruction. These two fables would seem to round out not only Thurber's book, but the story of man, to hint at hopelessness. The moral, "All men should strive to learn before they die what they are running from, and to, and why," however, contains the possibility of finding out, or at least the desirability of finding out. The scholarly lemming in the fable, the one who does not run, "shook his head sorrowfully, tore up what he had written through the years about his species, and started his studies all over again." But he did start again. The moral of "The Turtle Who Conquered Time" asks sadly, "Oh, why should the shattermyth have to be a crumplehope and a dampenglee?" There is some quality in these fables, and Thurber knows it because he put it there, that insists that the shattermyth can be something quite different from a crumplehope.

Indignations of a Senior Citizen

by John Updike

The appearance, in the yellow dust jacket that has become traditional, of one more collection of pieces by the late James Thurber
is a happy event, even for the reviewer obliged to report that the
bulk of the pieces are from his last years and as such tend to be
cranky, formless and lame. "The claw of the sea-puss," Thurber
once wrote (quoting F. Hopkinson Smith), "gets us all in the end";
and toward the end Thurber's humor was overwhelmed by puns and
dismay.

The puns are understandable. Blindness, in severing language
from the seen world of designated things, gives words a tyrannical
independence. Milton and Joyce wrung from verbal obsession a
special magnificence, and Thurber's late pieces, at their best—for
example, "The Tyranny of Trivia," collected in "Lanterns and
Lances"—do lead the reader deep into the wonderland of the al-
phabet and the dictionary. But in such weak rambles as, in this
collection, "The Lady from the Land" and "Carpe Noctem, If You
Can," logomachic tricks are asked to pass for wit and implausible
pun-swapping for human conversation.

As to the dismay: Mrs. Thurber, in her gracious and understated
introduction to this posthumous collection, defends her husband
against the charge of "bitterness and disillusion." But stories like
"The Future, If Any, of Comedy Or, Where Do We Non-Go from
Here?" and "Afternoon of a Playwright" do display, by way of
monologue in the ungainly disguise of dialogue, an irritation with
the present state of things so inclusive as to be pointless.

Television, psychoanalysis, the Bomb, the deterioration of grammar, the morbidity of contemporary literature—these were just a
few of Thurber's terminal pet peeves. The writer who had produced "Fables for Our Time" and "The Last Flower" out of the

thirties had become, by the end of the fifties, one more indignant senior citizen penning complaints about the universal decay of virtue.

The only oasis, in the dreadful world of post-midnight forebodings into which he had been plunged, is the Columbus, Ohio, of his boyhood, which he continued to remember "as fondly and sharply as a man on a sinking ship might remember his prairie home." In "Credos and Curios," for a few pages entitled "Return of the Native," his prose regains the crisp lucidity and glistening bias of "The Thurber Album." Then the dark tangled curtain falls again.

However, "Credos and Curios" should be cherished by every Thurberite for the seven random tributes he wrote, between 1938 and 1960, to seven artistic colleagues—Mary Petty, Elliott Nugent and five writers. His acute and sympathetic remarks on Scott Fitzgerald remind us that Thurber, too, was one of the curiously compact literary generation that came to birth in the twenties and whose passing has left the literary stage so strikingly empty. His affectionate memories of John McNulty and E. B. White, two friends who in their different ways achieved the literary tranquillity that eluded Thurber, better capture the spirit of New Yorker bonhomie than all "The Years with Ross."

His generous appreciation of Robert Benchley is most welcome of all, especially when taken as an antidote to the oddly curt paragraph with which *The New Yorker* noted the death, in 1949, of this remarkable artist. For if Thurber, whose international celebrity made him seem to loom unduly over the other American humorists of his vintage, is to be measured against his peers, the first name we strike is Benchley's. The surprising thing about Benchley is that he remains rereadable. His writings were so ephemeral they seem to defy being outdated; their utterly casual and innocent surface airily resists corrosion. I wonder how much of Thurber will weather so well.

His cartoons, of course, are incomparable; they dive into the depths of the dilemma that he felt beneath everything. Of the humorists of this century, he and Don Marquis were the most complex, the most pessimistic and the most ambitious. Thurber, in comparison to Marquis and Benchley, was not especially sensitive to the surface currents of American life, and as a journalist, uncomfortable, and, as a writer of straight fiction, unconvincing.

His great subject, springing from his physical disability, was what might be called the enchantment of misapprehension. His masterpieces, I think, are "My Life and Hard Times" and "The White Deer"—two dissimilar books alike in their beautiful evocation of a fluid chaos where communication is limited to wild, flitting gestures and where humans revolve and collide like glowing planets, lit solely from within, against a cosmic backdrop of gathering dark. Thurber's genius was to make of our despair a humorous fable. It is not surprising that such a gallant feat of equilibrium was not maintained to the end of his life.

Insomniac's Companion

by John Mortimer

Twenty years ago the works of James Thurber were thought of as the height of humour. It was never, if I remember the Blitz, possible to visit a bed-sitting-room that did not have, beside the *Horizons* and the *New Writings*, stuffed between the oatmeal-coloured elephant book-ends and beneath the reproduction Paul Nash, a Thurber, dog-eared from fire-watching, bent from the gasmask case. Being young, I was secretly mystified by the cult. The drawings seemed inept to me, as they did to Thurber, the closely written pages dull and occasionally arch. However, the adult aura was unassailable. How could we, nourished on tube-shelter tea and British Restaurant whale, not respond to the dry tinkle of ice in the highballs, the Battle of the Sexes, the Algonquin, and the reported wit of Robert Benchley? The mixture of sophistication and sent-up corn was irresistible. But so it has remained. Where other luxuries from the Age of Austerity, the life-plays of Christopher Fry, the death-films of Cocteau, have passed from fashion, Thurber remains part of the standard equipment of the British Intellectual. Walter Mitty is still responsible for two-thirds of our television drama. Also upon Thurber lies the heavy burden of having formed the style in which many dramatic critics write, with its wearily knowing air of having seen it all before and done better, and its reliance on puns: "Trivia Mundi has always been as dear to me as her bigger sister Gloria," or "Have gun, Will Shakespeare."

A long view of Thurber has now been made possible by the publication of two lavish volumes of his vintage works and two more Penguin selections. The amount he wrote seems immense, and indeed it is as a literary man, or as a man overawed by literature, that he makes his first impression. "Among the American writers I have stayed up with all night," he writes excitedly, "are Robert Bench-

"Insomniac's Companion" (review of *Vintage Thurber*) by John Mortimer. From *The New Statesman*, LXVII (January 10, 1964). Copyright © 1964 by *The New Statesman*. Reprinted by permission of *The New Statesman*.

ley, Heywood Broun, Scott Fitzgerald, Thomas Wolfe and Sinclair Lewis." He is greatly impressed by it all, and by *My Fair Lady, The Chalk Garden* and the novels of Henry James. Many of his pieces describe literary parties, ever an unpromising source of material, and much of his writing is composed of elaborate, sometimes laboured verbal games.

All of this is a pity, because what Thurber had, quarried for in these memorial tomes, started by being of great value. He was the poet laureate of insomnia. He knew exactly how mad anyone could go, faced with the terrifying prospect of a night's rest. He felt for the women who sit bolt upright every hour till dawn, cry "Hark" and throw their shoes down the passage to deter intruders. He understood the housewife who takes a shotgun to bed, convinced that, each night, the insurrection will break out. He is very good about his cousin Briggs Beall, who was afraid to stop breathing and had to have an alarm clock to wake him periodically so that he could make sure he was still alive. He was familiar with the tramping of ghosts, the endless, boring noise made by burglars which makes you feel that you ought to get up and help them to find the valuables. At his best Thurber touches on what seem to be the two great contradictory American terrors, that of sleeplessness and of large, predatory and highly sexed women.

The women in his drawings are well known to be shapeless, ugly, frenetic, throwing flowers in dionysian revelry, or crouched, ready to spring, at the ends of sofas. "They're playing 'Bolero,' Mr. Constantine. It drives me mad," "Have you forgotten our little suicide pact?" They form a world at war with the gentle, tolerant little men in pince-nez who find comfort only in large, friendly dogs. In a basic Thurber situation the man and the dog, clutching each other lovingly, are dancing to the radiogram. The savage wife-figure, glaring at them with her arms crossed, says: "Will you be good enough to dance outside?" The assumption is that men are smaller, more helpless and touching, than their galumphing mates; but they also have more wisdom. They alone can see the frightful black beast swooping down on them from the air. In the end they may turn and strangle their womenfolk at restaurant tables (and earn the gentle rebuke from the head waiter: "There's a place for that, sir"); or receive the symbolic baseball-bat of surrender from the Women's General.

The Thurber little man, short-sighted, put-upon creature, bruised and frightened by life, is appealing. The trouble is that he goes not at all with cocktails at the Algonquin; and perhaps the unease

with which I early greeted Thurber's work stems from a suspicion
that the "little man" may not have seemed entirely true to the author. In *The Years with Ross* Thurber tells a revealing story. He
was about to marry his sensible, attractive, charming and no doubt
not at all frightening second wife, Helen. As the *New Yorker's* editor, Ross sent Robert Benchley to him to put him off the idea of
marriage. With Thurber happily married, the Battle of the Sexes
might cease. In return, and as a practical joke, Thurber did one
drawing of a man and woman sailing happily together beneath the
stars. But this was not to be taken seriously. To the gratification of
the *New Yorker,* the war between men and women continued un-
abated. Not only was the put-upon little man quite different from
the tough, happy and sophisticated artist bearded by Bob Benchley
in his suite at the Royalton, but his sufferings were a standing joke
kept up for the readers of the *New Yorker*—just as the fiction of
the unpleasantness of mothers-in-law is preserved for the audiences
at holiday camps in Shoeburyness. So the Battle of the Sexes comes
to appear part of the Great American dream, something longed for,
in those glossy *New Yorker* pages, but no more substantial than that
watch from Cartier's or the nest egg in the Chase National Bank.

Perhaps that is why, read in this great bulk, the humour of Thurber comes to wear so thin. The creators of "Little Men" are ever
in a spot. From the heights of Switzerland and his genius Chaplin
now speaks of the "Little Fellow" he once was with wistful aliena-
tion. In the same way the small, bumbling Thurber innocent came
less and less to represent anything his author felt, and resort was
had to the whimsy of the fairy-tales, the animals and the Last
Flower. And that's why the best pieces are still about Thurber's
youth. Better far the nights spent in hilarious insomnia with his
parents and his cousin Briggs Beall than those latter-day carouses
in the distinguished company of Robert Benchley, Heywood Broun,
Scott Fitzgerald, Thomas Wolfe and Sinclair Lewis.

Decline and Fall

by Jesse Bier

Working in both the pre-World War II and post-World War II periods and adequately reflecting both sides of that second great watershed of American morale, James Thurber is the logical figure with whom to begin modern judgments. Since the critical question is one of decline or resurgence, we shall proceed accordingly, evaluating themes and techniques as they directly bear upon that discussion and centering Thurber at the outset and conclusion.

Two works of Thurber give us the most convenient measure of his career. Side by side with *Fables for Our Time* (1940) we can place counterparts from *Further Fables for Our Time* (1956). The difference between "The Owl Who Thought He Was God," reversing Lincoln's proverbialism, and the later "The Rose and the Weed" is instructive.

> In a country garden a lovely rose looked down upon a common weed and said, "You are an unwelcome guest, economically useless, and unsightly of appearance. The Devil must love weeds, he made so many of them."
>
> The unwelcome guest looked up at the rose and said, "Lilies that fester smell far worse than weeds, and, one supposes, that goes for roses."
>
> "My name is Dorothy Perkins," the rose said haughtily. "What are you—a beetleweed, a bladderweed, a beggarweed? The names of weeds are ugly." And Dorothy shuddered slightly, but lost none of her pretty petals.

The Rose and the Weed continue their argument, which the Rose wishes to end by citing Shakespearian references to herself.

> Just then, and before Miss Perkins could recite, a wind came out of the west, riding low to the ground and swift, like the cavalry of March, and Dorothy Perkins' beautiful disdain suddenly be-

came a scattering of petals, economically useless, and of appearance not especially sightly. The weed stood firm, his head to the wind, armored, or so he thought, in security and strength, but as he was brushing a few rose petals and aphids from his lapels, the hand of the gardener flashed out of the air and pulled him out of the ground by the roots before you could say Dorothy Perkins, or, for that matter, jewelweed.

> *Moral: Tout, as the French say, in a philosophy older than ours and an idiom often more succinct, passe.*

The reversal is now compounded and total. There is the momentary though telling subversion of Lincoln, but the point is now incidental to Thurber's complete misanthropy. Even the acidic Ambrose Bierce would have perversely sided with the aristocratic rose, in simple reversalism; Thurber goes the whole distance. And in the barroom fable, "The Truth About Toads," every animal present owns his desperate pride, even the toad, who thinks he has a precious jewel in his head (a "toadpaz," mocks the bartender). When the Woodpecker opens the toad's head, there isn't "anything there, gleaming or lovely or precious." And Thurber's moral is "Open most heads and you will find nothing shining, not even a mind." This new explicitness and hardness exceed even Bierce's fables ("Man and Goose," for instance) and govern Thurber's last work, replete with its accentuated and uncompromising pessimism. The key to a now developed misanthropy lies in the contrast between the excluded, saving minority of some doubters in "The Owl," a red fox, a humble dormouse, and a French poodle, and the general inclusiveness of his attack in the newer fable.

Moreover, punning is almost the only device Thurber is left with, a noteworthy technical contrast to the greater number of devices used before, even in stringent pieces like "The Owl" and "The Shrike" and "The Unicorn." What distinguished the earlier pieces was a greater playfulness and the joy of variation he had been patient enough to practice. In the later work his repetitions and overextensions are technical counterparts of a moral decline and bitterness.

In his extremism he pushes the antiproverbialist and antirhetorical qualities he always had to absolute limits. There is no communication at all possible in the comic misapprehensions of language that he dramatizes. And that leads him to the defeatism figured in the connivance and stupidity of "The Daws" and to the nihilism of his concluding fable, "The Shore and the Sea."

There are still comic attempts at literalism, comic metaphor, and confusionism, to be sure, along with the now obsessive punning. But his disabusement, barely and cannily saved from diatribe by these last comic gestures, is comprehensive and deep—and, at the last, not very funny.

In the last stage of his career, a number of targets that he and his *New Yorker* colleagues had chosen for special assault are recognizable. The misogyny is still active. "I like to do what I can," he confesses to *Life*, "to keep the American woman—my great mortal enemy—in excellent condition for the fight." He shares in comedy's attack on children in *The Saturday Review*.

> "The trouble with you is, you just don't like no children," she said coldly.
> "You are wrong, madame," I said icily. "I *do* like no children."

He struck at Madison Avenue rhetoric repeatedly. But he also turned more and more to the unparticularized subject of the world's madness. "I think there's been a fallout of powdered fruitcake—everyone's going nuts." To a large extent he moved away from special concrete subjects of attack, and he turned either to general assault upon humanity or to an ingrown preoccupation with deteriorating language. In his more vehement mood, "The Bat Who Got the Hell Out" stands in clear contrast not only to his own earlier pieces but to a similar fable of George Ade, "The Good People Who Rallied to the Support of the Church." The contrast is not merely between a modern forcefulness and an earlier gentleness, but between the misanthropic invective of one age and the partial sympathy of an earlier time. Thurber's last stage represents a retreat from humor. And his irritabilities, his explicitness, his animus, his borderline perversities and grotesqueries, his final hopelessness, and his ingrownness are indices to the whole contemporary epoch, not only to his own career.

He touched philosophically on the general matter when he commented once on the unfunniness of fun in our time and, indeed, on the unfunny meanings we now place upon the word "funny," e.g., ominous ("there's a funny sound in the motor"), disturbing, scary. He recognized an age's declension to fright and horrors and the consequent degeneration of our sense of humor.[1] In this regard,

---

1 He told his colleague, E. B. White, that a humorist was like a surgeon. His terminology was both ultimate and curative, but he had less and less recourse to such self-characterization as time went on. His own undertakings were more mortuary, as if he understood that the patient was dead and he consented to sign the last certificates.

he might have remembered how "comic" books became horror comics in the late forties and fifties and how his own humorous *New Yorker* published one of the most horrific pieces of journalism ever printed, John Hersey's *Hiroshima* (as it, still later, published Capote's *In Cold Blood* in its entirety).

C. S. Holmes has made the best case for a continuously vital Thurber. But Holmes's concessions, for example, to Thurber's growing anger and didacticism, have a way of being leading ones. And when the apologist elaborates Thurber's opposition of a masculine fantasy principle, loving and peaceable, to a female reality principle, cold and hostile, the defense disconcerts us. For such misogyny has become indeed too systematized and unhealthy in Thurber; he moved from his attack on certain women, on American women, to an onslaught on women in general and into a war on reality. And in his tightened equation of fantasy with honorific male idiosyncrasy and confusionism, he capitulated not only to a final grandiose oversimplification but to frank neurosis. Comic social criticism is possible on grounds that are more sophisticated and less extreme than that.

But Thurber increasingly withdraws from outer subjects anyway and seeks his comedy in anagrammatical humor and word play. He still enjoys antiproverbialism, getting his effect from changing or omitting single letters: "There's no business like shoe business," or "Don, give up the ship." But his efforts are less and less inspired and are largely predictable or flat: "A stitch in time saves none." Becoming blind, he compensates in comedy of overintricate verbal play and of a predominantly auditory cast, as in the manufactured compounds of his later definitions. "A Fussgrape: 1. . . . a light eater . . . a scornmuffin, a shuncabbage. 2. . . . one who boasts of his knowledge of wines, a smugbottle." This is the intermittent cuteness to which his old sustained ingenuity is reduced. Almost a generation before, in "Ladies' and Gentlemen's Guide to Modern English Usage" (*The Owl in the Attic*, 1931), he had sustained exquisite comedy in the grammatical confusions of "who," "which," the correct use of "the subjunctive," etc. But in every case his demonstrations were actually rescued by his supplying the right and unaffected style to employ and a common-sensical tact. That implicit hopefulness disappears and, with it, his capacity for situational and sustained humor along with the verbal confusion. He is led to strained punning, insistent alliteration, or general intellectual gamesmanship in his last stage. "We battle for the word where the very Oedipus of reason crumbles beneath us." He becomes our comic Joyce, likewise degenerating into a fascination with ingrown verbal resources. It is his final refuge.

In "The Last Clock" [2] he presents a garbled fragment, as Holmes admits, of a second-rate, nineteenth-century poet, Longfellow, celebrating optimism as the world ends . . . again strained and, as it were, fixated. His satire on the exquisite breakdown of communication, itself a leading cause and symptom of a vaster breakdown, is undercut by his use of Longfellow. The disrupted communication is not worth having anyway. And so he finds himself without a true position to take.

Having himself celebrated disorder and illogicality in the face of overorganized modern life, Thurber at the last champions ordered and adult communication. But he loses his own clarity in the process, his own larger, braver coherence. And he loses his revelry. He withdraws to mere cleverness. He is so disaffected or dug in, overgeneralized or introverted, and both together, that it appears as if he has come over that epochal watershed of World War II as in a barrel over a moral Niagara. Both the vehicle and the man are staved through.

Still, Thurber had gone on trying, and there was a certain pertinacity and courage in that. The recognition puts us in an anomalous position about the whole era as well as Thurber. We find ourselves acknowledging talent while we indict it. What is the essence of the matter if we shall be passing such ambiguous but fell judgment on an age as well as a man?

What we have is a highly diversified group working in a period that is itself a kind of historical anticlimax, the long cold war after hot war. How can they attain or maintain heights in a period that is itself a prolonged repercussion to climactic breakdown, a sick joke of history? We will discover comic tenacities everywhere, as, indeed, in Thurber, and be prompted to think of resurgence. But the intransigent evidence argues for net decline and even decadence on all sides. The strains and grotesqueries of the later Thurber are also apparent in other contemporary authors, in a host of fellow cartoonists, especially those who treat the outré in full abandon, in the efflorescence of sick humor in this period, our own latter-day

[2] The word "last" becomes obsessive in his final works (as in "The Last Flower" also). Clocks and all machines, especially sensitive ones, fail us at last. And "flowers," an even more repetitive image of pathetic doom, are plucked or otherwise destroyed at last judgments. Beauty and fragile life are overcome, as vital speech is, and a pensive nihilism informs his whole concluding view.

Baudelaireism, in comic enfeeblements and excesses on the air and on the screen, and in the uncertain position of Jewish humor in this period. If there are exceptions and resurgences, as there clearly are, they appear as yet insufficient to counter the evidence for the decline and even fall of American humor. Such judgment is impersonal and pragmatic. In the material before us corroborations are alternately subtle and notoriously flagrant.

Thurber the Talker

by Peter De Vries

In the first year of my marriage, in the winter of 1944, I was destined to have a smoothly running domestic life disrupted by a honeymoon, delayed from the time when my finances had not permitted it and when I had been pressed by the duties of a job which had, in fact, made the union ludicrous from the first. I was working then for *Poetry* magazine. Editorial toils on that monthly regularly alternated with time-outs to beg, borrow or bludgeon our tiny salaries out of civic-minded patrons. I say civic-minded because Chicago has always been proud of *Poetry's* deficit. The magazine's annual critical financial illness was always reported in the newspapers somewhere near the obituary page.

James Thurber knew all about this, and so when I asked him to come give us a benefit lecture he did not dismiss the idea out of hand, did not decline, without a hearing, the rigors of a cross-country trip and the horrors of the public platform. After some oblique, tentative correspondence on the subject, we agreed to meet in New York, where my wife and I accordingly decided to spend our postponed honeymoon, of which a meeting with Thurber thus became an unexpected highlight.

We were greeted by Thurber in his East Side apartment in the late afternoon. Seeing him pick his way through the dusky foyer with his arms out like the feelers of an insect made me remember a line of poetry I had read in another little magazine years before, by an author whose name I had forgotten. It was the last sentence of a poem to Hart Crane, ending with some conceit or other about Crane's ultimate esthetic essence reducing itself at last to a single naked nerve, "stripped to slide across the pumice of eternity." I thought that Thurber might be likely to slide across the pumice of eternity a little longer than Hart Crane, probably as long, say, as

Lewis Carroll, but of course such speculations are vain, and this one is recalled chiefly as an instance of the sort of glimmery caprices he inspired as well as indulged in.

We soon settled down to cases, and it was a few months later, on an April day in Chicago, that we met again, this time in a room at the Ambassador East, to make final arrangements for the plan we had hit on in his New York apartment for lightening the miseries of public speech.

It was a rather shabby little stratagem that we had cooked up. Thurber had declined to give a formal lecture but would not mind answering questions. To make it even more foolproof, I myself made up the questions the audience would ask: questions for which the remarks he was smoothly and eloquently getting off in the relaxation of the hotel room—about men, women, dogs—would serve beautifully as answers. It would be as simple as putting nickels in a jukebox, and as painless for him. It was a quiz show in reverse. I scribbled down the queries, hastily tailoring them to fit the gems dropping from his lips. I wrote all these questions out in advance on slips of paper of different sizes, shapes and even colors, to bolster the fiction that they had just been jotted down by members of the audience.

The event was held on a Saturday morning in the Arts Club, located in that pastry chef's dream, the Wrigley Building. What any veteran of Thurber's conversation would have known would happen, happened. With the first question he took the bit between his teeth and galloped off on as fine a formal lecture as the audience had ever heard, and they had heard Frank Lloyd Wright, Robert Penn Warren and Rudolph Ganz.

When I had called for him at the hotel, an hour before, he had given me a hand to shake as clammy as my own. Now, face to face with the invisible cloud of patrons, he underwent the transformation he always did in a pinch, because the phenomenon known as Thurber had two contradictory sides: apprehension and mastery of any given situation. There was no element in human life to whose hazards he was not attuned, or of which he was not in firm control. I am sure that the slender and attractive wife who walked by his side in support of her blind charge, then and for the next 17 years, drew from the hand that clutched her arm some sort of strength in return for what she gave. There was some companionate, two-way current between them which they alone knew to its depths. At any rate, at the Arts Club he had them eating out of that hand inside of five minutes. The bundle of nerves was a tower of strength.

I sidled unobtrusively backstage, where I crumpled and dropped into the nearest wastebasket the slips of paper and let Thurber give account of that gift he displayed to the last in private: that of one of the great monologists of our time. He was a storyteller, mimic, fantasist, realist, running commentator and mine of information on every subject under the sun. As writer, man of letters, artist and *bête curieuse,* he was, of course, one of the specialties of our time. He never to my knowledge mounted a public platform again, but he occupied that one just long enough to show that he might have borne comparison with Mark Twain on that score too, had he cared to add it to his list of accomplishments.

People have different versions of what Thurber reminded them of. Some say a cricket. Some a bird. Some say one of his own dogs. He always put me in mind of a praying mantis. About his elongated form there hovered the same air of something delicate and improbable, of almost eerie sensitivity, of tactile grace and predatory caution; and, of course, the same catholic interest in everything as potential prey, for the name of that myth- and legend-haunted insect is inaccurate by one letter. Thurber's forepaws, too, lay folded in repose only when they were not tearing something to shreds, be it a handkerchief, the sash of a dressing gown or a personified tendency of modern life. For he loved midnight wrangles and the good, pugnacious sociability of Tim Costello's saloon as much as he did the word games and old song titles with which he outwitted the laudanum hour and whiled away the long stretches of insomnia. . . .

Thurber was equally good at self-disparagement. Since his foibles were among the best of our time, there was something universal, something larger than life in the self he pounced on for our amusement and instruction—something at once acutely contemporary and abidingly human. Thus his humor performed supremely the office of that precarious art, which is to keep ourselves in focus, in perspective and in balance. For all this, and so much more, we and our successors can be grateful to old Jim Thurber and his very keen vision.

Antic Disposition

by W. J. Weatherby

There were no dogs, not even floppy bloodhounds, in the London hotel room. James Thurber sat alone, his four senses so active that our five felt disgraced. His eyes did not look blind behind his glasses, they had not got that look of eyes washed in milk that many blind people's have, and he found his whisky and his cigarettes unerringly: a real "pro" at overcoming the handicaps of blindness as at everything else.

Some of Thurber's fans might have expected to find a Seeing Eye dog reposing at his feet, those fans—or nonreaders as Thurber might call them—who think of dogs and Thurber as inseparable. Thurber himself feels as though he is dogged by his dogs. People who meet him gush about how much they love his "charming dogs" and his "lovely cartoons," while the gloomy social critic, the superb prose writer, fumes behind his glasses, behind the little moustache that seems to bristle with indignation.

He looks like one of his own characters, "My Life and Hard Times" 20 years later: a tall, lean man thinned down by the worry of the war between men and women, his moustache an overcivilised patch that any caveman would scorn. But he does not talk like a Thurber man: his talk is a constant stream that in 66 years must have added up to a whole sea, for Thurber is one of the greatest talkers in America. It seems incredible that he has had the time to write such a large and varied body of work as well—and he writes slowly, a rebuke to the satisfied-first-time school. He calls himself not a writer but a "re-writer": the finished book lies somewhere between the fifth and fifteenth versions, the prose style by then giving an impression of effortlessness but without any hint of glibness. . . .

Blind and unable to see his words, he composes in his head—

that memory again—and continually fears that sloppiness may creep back while he is not looking. A reporter who created a modern prose style—this evolution seems one of his greatest achievements. His view of the world is thus admirably expressed, that view of a twentieth-century man gripped in a panic that drives him into all kinds of odd antics. The quick reader sees the antics and thinks Thurber a funny man—"a clown," as he says bitterly. Underneath, of course, there is often as much pessimism as in Faulkner. And in conversation what he says is often deeply gloomy, and yet—like his work—is expressed with such verve and pell-mell vitality that the final impression is optimistic, of a man engaged in life to the hilt, whose desperation comes from seeing so many missed opportunities for living.

He certainly has not missed many himself. Blind in his left eye since boyhood, totally blind for the last ten years, he has added acting to a long list of activities and has come over to London to write a book or two, a play or two, and to repeat his Broadway performance in "The Thurber Carnival." And of course to talk. That day in the London hotel he needed hardly any questions, pouring out what seemed like part of the interior monologue that has been going on now for 66 years:

"All Americans are going 600 miles an hour jet-propelled. But where to? I know one man who is so afraid of being alone that he takes a portable radio to the bathroom. They ask me what I do in a room just sitting there and when I say, 'Meditate,' they think I need a psychiatrist. . . ."

Interviewer: "I heard you sometimes write at parties—."

Thurber: "That's right. Helen will come up and say, 'Thurber, stop writing. That girl has been talking to you for ten minutes and you never even realised she was there.' I have to admit I was preoccupied because I had just realised how to get out of a certain paragraph. People seem to think I'm just a funny man, a dog man. I haven't done any drawings since I went blind but they still ask me how my dogs are coming along. Some people even think I make jokes about dogs. For God's sake anybody who looks at my drawings with enough observation should be able to see the dogs play the part of intelligence and repose. Typical of the stupidity of our own species was my woman who said, 'If I rang the wrong number, why did you answer the phone?' That seems typical of the female intelligence, though I do get some intelligent letters from women. Notice the despair and resignation of the dog in that picture. Oh, I've been writing about the ego for 30 years and I'm still taken for a clown. . . .

"You know—there I go now—people talk about a blind person being in the dark but he really lives in a suffusion of light. That's what I say in my new book—it's lighter than you think. Don't look back in anger or forward with foreboding, look around in awareness—if you can. But people just develop a TV mouth and a TV stare. They don't read. Walter Lippmann said on TV some weeks ago that he didn't feel the world was coming apart. Well, that's one man's opinion. I think we are in a terrible state. We have a new theory that Columbus didn't want to discover the New World, he just wanted to get the hell out of this one. I say these things and people just talk about my 'charming dogs' or my cartoons. . . .

". . . You know—there's another 'you know'—I'm going to be busy over here. The greatest hyphen link—that's what I call the Anglo-American world. The British and the Americans have always argued like a family, but the most important thing in our world is for us to stick together. . . ."

When he mentioned a name he would carefully spell it; his monologue itself sometimes seemed like an act of courtesy to save a fellow newspaperman from having to ask any questions. One tried a question or two, but they were like logs swept away down a flooding river, the answers appearing minutes and many paragraphs later. When at last the Thurber monologue paused, one said goodbye with thanks for the chance to tune in on it. He beamed and when last seen was sitting back on the couch. Had he started writing again?

Thurber: Man Against Monster

by Paul Jennings

Thurber had no more passionate admirers than his English ones, possibly because that specifically American wryness did not produce in America quite the same shock of delighted surprise as it did here in the thirties and forties. We had read writers like Mark Twain; but Thurber somehow gave us a sense of revelation. Here it was, a new kind of wit in a perfected literary form.

Many people, if they thought of the man in those early days, must have envisaged someone vaguely unathletic, permanently middle-aged, endomorphic, something between Walter Mitty and the strange boneless men, apprehensively staring, mouths glumly turned down, of his drawings. (Thurber relates in his book on Ross how E. B. White, catching him in an attempt to make his drawings look more three-dimensional, said: "Don't do that. If you ever got good you'd be mediocre.")

Committed to Man

But when, later, we *saw* Thurber on his frequent post-war visits to England, we found someone very different: neat but restless, slim, upright, elderly, an ectomorph. Above all, Thurber was a precisian. He was always restlessly building neat walls against Old Chaos. His humour was the first that could be regarded as a genuine literary product of an age in which the ordinary man, heir to centuries of peasant and family life, suddenly (for art telescopes these processes) is up against the fragmentation, complexity, and directionless menace of industrial civilisation.

The menace is clearer now, not to be met with the delicate indirectness of humour. Lesser people can turn this into a formula, saying: "Look at me, I'm the Little Man against civilisation." But

"Thurber: Man Against Monster" by Paul Jennings. From *The Observer*, November 5, 1961, p. 10. Copyright © 1961, *The Observer*, London. Reprinted by permission of the publisher.

Thurber was far too worried and driven by it to have time to stop and make that kind of formulation.

He was Committed, in a very much deeper sense than that commonly denoted by the word. He was committed to Man, and his enemy was a kind of shifting monster of Inaccuracy—whether the moral inaccuracy of scientific lunacy, the inaccuracy of people's knowledge about each other, or the inaccuracy of the misremembered quotation (he had total recall and never forgot anything. The last time I met him, at the Stafford Hotel in London, he was wondering whether Whitehead, the philosopher, could have been any good at all because of a misquotation he had made).

Another frequent form of the enemy was inaccuracy in English construction, about which there are some splendid explosions in "Lanterns and Lances," his last book ("a woman came chattering into my dreams, saying, 'We can sleep 20 people in this house in a pinch, but we can only eat 12.' "). It is not surprising that his great literary hero was Henry James.

By the Alarm Clock

Thurber's style took some time forming. He was born in 1894, and after Ohio State University he had several years in journalism. On the *Columbus Dispatch* he found news stories in citizens like the one who received a radio programme on the steel rims of his spectacles. In France, after unsuccessful attempts at a novel, he was assistant editor of the Riviera edition of the *Chicago Tribune*. By 1926 he was back in America, on the *New York Evening Post*. After many rejections he then got a piece into the *New Yorker*, written in a 45-minute period for which his wife had set the alarm clock, saying he spent too much time on his articles.

Words were *things* to Thurber, and this became more and more evident as blindness descended on him during the last quarter of his life. He could see the whole thing hanging up there in his mind, he just went on restlessly choosing the words. Perfectly-fashioned pieces came out, showing an innocent dreamland, where there was no confusion or inaccuracy, only joy.

He sought and gave joy in the theatre, too (although, as he once said to me, "I'm not long on plot, you know"). We must always regret the collapse of the London plans for the stage version of "The Thurber Carnival," in which he appeared personally with great success.

It is hard to think he is gone, even though the climate of his work grows larger and more inviting all the time. He created a *genre* and was a giant in it. In a century's time, critics may acknowledge Walter Mitty as a basic twentieth-century figure. If Faust is pure intellect and Don Juan is pure sense, Mitty is pure fantasy. It is fitting that the native city of the man who gave form to the Mitty-idea—this wonderfully new, big, true discovery—should be Columbus.

James Thurber

by E. B. White

I was one of the lucky ones; I knew him before blindness hit him, before fame hit him, and I tend always to think of him as a young artist in a small office in a big city, with all the world still ahead. It was a fine thing to be young and at work in New York for a new magazine when Thurber was young and at work, and I will always be glad that this happened to me.

It was fortunate that we got on well; the office we shared was the size of a hall bedroom. There was just room enough for two men, two typewriters, and a stack of copy paper. The copy paper disappeared at a scandalous rate—not because our production was high (although it was) but because Thurber used copy paper as the natural receptacle for discarded sorrows, immediate joys, stale dreams, golden prophecies, and messages of good cheer to the outside world and to fellow-workers. His mind was never at rest, and his pencil was connected to his mind by the best conductive tissue I have ever seen in action. The whole world knows what a funny man he was, but you had to sit next to him day after day to understand the extravagance of his clowning, the wildness and subtlety of his thinking, and the intensity of his interest in others and his sympathy for their dilemmas—dilemmas that he instantly enlarged, put in focus, and made immortal, just as he enlarged and made immortal the strange goings on in the Ohio home of his boyhood. His waking dreams and his sleeping dreams commingled shamelessly and uproariously. Ohio was never far from his thoughts, and when he received a medal from his home state in 1953, he wrote, "The clocks that strike in my dreams are often the clocks of Columbus." It is a beautiful sentence and a revealing one.

He was both a practitioner of humor and a defender of it. The day he died, I came on a letter from him, dictated to a secretary and signed in pencil with his sightless and enormous "Jim." "Every time is a time for humor," he wrote. "I write humor the way a surgeon operates, because it is a livelihood, because I have a great urge to do it, because many interesting challenges are set up, and because I have the hope it may do some good." Once, I remember, he heard someone say that humor is a shield, not a sword, and it made him mad. He wasn't going to have anyone beating his sword into a shield. That "surgeon," incidentally, is pure Mitty. During his happiest years, Thurber did not write the way a surgeon operates, he wrote the way a child skips rope, the way a mouse waltzes.

Although he is best known for "Walter Mitty" and "The Male Animal," the book of his I like best is "The Last Flower." In it you will find his faith in the renewal of life, his feeling for the beauty and fragility of life on earth. Like all good writers, he fashioned his own best obituary notice. Nobody else can add to the record, much as he might like to. And of all the flowers, real and figurative, that will find their way to Thurber's last resting place, the one that will remain fresh and wiltproof is the little flower he himself drew, on the last page of that lovely book.

Chronology of Important Dates

1894   James Grover Thurber born to Mary Fisher Thurber and Charles L. Thurber, December 8, in Columbus, Ohio.

1901   Thurber blinded in left eye when accidentally shot by an arrow while playing cowboys and Indians with his brothers.

1909–13   Writes Class Prophecy for eighth grade at Douglas School which anticipates "The Secret Life of Walter Mitty." Enters East High. Shy, gangling, badly dressed, but recognized as clever by classmates. Elected president of senior class, 1913.

1913   Enters Ohio State University. Lonely and unnoticed for two years. 1914–15, drops out, but does not tell parents.

1915–16   Returns to university. Meets Elliott Nugent, who befriends him, spruces him up, gets him into fraternity, and encourages him to join campus activities.

1917–18   He and Nugent write for student paper, *The Ohio State Lantern,* and for the humor magazine, *The Sun-Dial.* Takes course in the novel from Professor Joseph Russell Taylor which confirms him as "a Henry James man" for life.

1918   Editor of *The Sun-Dial.* Leaves in June without graduating and gets post as code clerk at the embassy in Paris.

1918–20   Sees Paris through Jamesian eyes. Writes enthusiastic letters to Nugent.

1920   Back to Columbus and job as reporter for the Columbus *Dispatch.* Begins writing and directing musical comedies for the Scarlet Mask Club of Ohio State, and acting and directing at The Strollers club, the university drama society.

1922   Marries Althea Adams, Ohio State beauty queen, whom he had met at The Strollers.

1923   *Dispatch* gives him his own Sunday column, "Credos and Curios."

1924   At the urging of Althea, leaves *Dispatch* to try fortunes as free-lance writer.

1925   Off to France with Althea, to write novel, which he never finished. Gets job on Paris edition of Chicago *Tribune,* and in December, on Riviera edition, published in Nice.

1926   Back to U. S. Tries unsuccessfully to sell parody of popular science books titled *Why We Behave Like Microbe Hunters.* Goes to work as reporter for the New York *Evening Post.* Bombards the newly founded *New Yorker* with humorous sketches. All rejected.

1927   Finally sells *New Yorker* two poems and a piece about a man in a revolving door. Meets E. B. White at a party in Greenwich Village. White introduces him to Harold Ross, who hires him not as writer but as managing editor. Finally convinces Ross he is a writer, not an editor.

1929   Collaborates with E. B. White on *Is Sex Necessary?* Best-seller.

1931   First drawings appear in *New Yorker. The Owl in the Attic and Other Perplexities.* Daughter Rosemary born, October 7.

1932   *The Seal in the Bedroom.*

1933   *My Life and Hard Times.* Dwight MacDonald calls it the best book of humor to come out of the postwar period.

1934   One-man show of drawings at the Valentine Gallery, New York.

1935   Divorced from Althea. Marries Helen Wismer. *The Middle-Aged Man on the Flying Trapeze.* Charles Poore describes Thurber as "a Joyce in false-face" (*The New York Times,* November 24, 1935).

1937   To England and France. One-man show at the Storran Gallery, London. *Let Your Mind Alone.* David Garnett calls Thurber "the most original and humorous writer living."

1939   *The Last Flower.* "The Secret Life of Walter Mitty" appears in *The New Yorker,* XV (March 18, 1939), 19–20. Begins to have eye trouble.

1940   *The Male Animal* opens at the Cort Theater, New York, January 9. *Fables for Our Time and Famous Poems Illustrated.*

1940–41   Series of eye operations and progressive loss of sight. Nervous crack-up, summer of 1941.

1942   *My World—and Welcome to It. The Male Animal* filmed, with Henry Fonda, Olivia de Havilland, and Jack Carson.

1943   *Men, Women and Dogs* and *Many Moons.*

1944   *The Great Quillow.* One-man show of drawings at Princeton University, Cornell University, and the Arts Club of Chicago. At the invitation of Peter De Vries, Thurber gives his only public lecture, for the benefit of *Poetry,* in Chicago.

1945   *The Thurber Carnival* brings general recognition of Thurber's importance as a writer. *The White Deer.* First signs of stylistic shift from "eye-writing" to "ear-writing."

1947   Samuel Goldwyn stars Danny Kaye in film version of "The Secret Life of Walter Mitty." Thurber unhappy with the result.

1948   *The Beast in Me and Other Animals.*

1950   Turns down offer of honorary degree from Ohio State University because of gag rule on visiting speakers imposed by trustees. Accepts honorary Doctor of Letters degree from Kenyon College instead.

1951   Honorary degree from Williams College. Last drawing—self-portrait for cover of July 9 issue of *Time.*

1952   *The Thurber Album.*

1953   Honorary degree from Yale. Accepting Sesquicentennial Medal from the Ohioana Library Association, speaks out for humor as force for social good in a time of fear and suspicion. *Thurber Country.*

1955   Visits France and England. Interviewed by Plimpton and Steele for *The Paris Review* "Art of Fiction" series.

1956   *Further Fables for Our Time* dedicated to Elmer Davis. Interviewed by Alistair Cooke on *Omnibus* TV program.

1957   *Further Fables* awarded American Library Association's Liberty and Justice Award. *The Wonderful O* and *Alarms and Diversions.*

1958   Visits England and is the first American since Mark Twain to be invited by the editors of *Punch* to carve his initials on the table, along with those of Thackeray and other notables of the past.

1959   *The Years with Ross.*

1960   *A Thurber Carnival* opens at the ANTA Theater, New York, February 26. Wins Antoinette Perry Award for distinguished writing. In September, Thurber fulfills lifelong ambition and joins cast for eighty-eight performances. Takes part in dedication ceremonies at opening of Denney Hall, the new humanities building at Ohio State.

1961   *Lanterns and Lances.* Visits England; interviewed constantly. Suffers stroke, October 4. Rallies after surgery, but stricken with pneumonia and dies, November 2. Buried in Columbus. Last words reputedly, "God bless . . . God damn."

1962   *Credos and Curios* published posthumously.

Notes on the Editor and Contributors

CHARLES S. HOLMES is Professor of English at Pomona College, in Claremont, California. He is the author of *The Clocks of Columbus: The Literary Career of James Thurber.*

The late W. H. AUDEN (died 1973), distinguished British-born poet and critic, whose *The Age of Anxiety* gave a name to the post-World War II era, was a Thurber admirer of long standing. His most recent book is a collection of essays, *Forewords and Afterwords.*

JESSE BIER is Professor of English at the University of Montana. He is the author of two books of fiction as well as the historical study, *The Rise and Fall of American Humor.*

WALTER BLAIR, Professor Emeritus at the University of Chicago, is an authority on the history of American humor. Among his books are *Native American Humor* and *Horse Sense in American Humor.*

MICHAEL BURNETT is Assistant Professor of English at Fairhaven College, in Bellingham, Washington.

ROBERT M. COATES, who died in 1973, was a staff member and contributor to *The New Yorker* for many years. He is the author of *The Bitter Season, Wisteria Cottage,* and *The Hour After Westerly and Other Stories.*

MALCOLM COWLEY, noted critic and writer, specializes in twentieth-century American literature. Among his most influential books are *Exile's Return* and *The Literary Situation.* He is the editor of *The Portable Faulkner* and of *The Stories of F. Scott Fitzgerald.*

PETER DE VRIES, novelist, playwright, and humorist, is a member of *The New Yorker* editorial staff. His many books include *The Tunnel of Love, The Blood of the Lamb,* and his recent collection of essays, *Without a Stitch in Time.*

ROBERT H. ELIAS is Professor of English at Cornell University. He is the author of *Theodore Dreiser, Apostle of Nature* and *Entangling Alliances with None,* a study of the American twenties.

DAVID GARNETT, British author and critic, is best known for his story, "Lady into Fox." He was one of the first critics to take Thurber seriously as a writer.

PAUL JENNINGS, British humorist and essayist, is the author of *Oddly Enough, It's an Odd Thing, But. . . .*, and many other books of humor.

ROBERT E. MORSBERGER is the author of *James Thurber*, the first book-length study of Thurber, and is presently at work on a biography of General Lew Wallace. He is Professor of English at California Polytechnic University, in Pomona, California.

JOHN MORTIMER, barrister and man of letters, writes frequently for *The New Statesman*.

DOROTHY PARKER, who died in 1967, was one of the great wits of the twenties and thirties, and a central figure in the famous Algonquin Round Table group. A poet and short-story writer, she was one of the early contributors to *The New Yorker*.

GEORGE PLIMPTON is one of the original editors of *The Paris Review*, and MAX STEELE is a member of its editorial board. Together they helped develop the series of interviews with living authors which has been one of the outstanding features of the magazine.

JOHN SEELYE is Professor of English at the University of Connecticut. He is the author of *Melville: The Ironic Diagram; The True Adventures of Huckleberry Finn, As Told By John Seelye;* and a novel, *The Kid.* He is a frequent contributor to *The New Republic* and other journals.

EDWARD STONE, Professor of English at Ohio University, is the author of *The Battle and the Books: Some Aspects of Henry James* and *A Certain Morbidness: A View of American Literature.*

RICHARD C. TOBIAS is Professor of English at the University of Pittsburgh. He is the author of *The Art of James Thurber.*

JOHN UPDIKE, short-story writer, novelist, and poet, is the author of such well-known books as *Rabbit, Run; The Centaur,* and *Couples.* He is a frequent contributor to *The New Yorker.*

GERALD WEALES is Professor of English at the University of Pennsylvania. He is the author of *Religion in Modern English Drama, American Drama Since World War II,* and the children's story, *Miss Grimsbee Is a Witch.*

W. J. WEATHERBY, British journalist and critic, contributes frequently to *The Guardian.*

E. B. WHITE, of *The New Yorker,* is the author of such well-known books as *One Man's Meat, Charlotte's Web,* and *The Second Tree from the Corner.*

NORRIS YATES, Professor of English at Iowa State University, is the author of *William T. Porter and "The Spirit of the Times," The American Humorist: Conscience of the Twentieth Century,* and *Robert Benchley.*

Selected Bibliography

The definitive bibliography of Thurber's work, including his drawings, is Edwin T. Bowden's *James Thurber: A Bibliography* (Columbus, Ohio: The Ohio State University Press, 1968).

There are useful bibliographies of critical and biographical materials in Robert E. Morsberger's *James Thurber* (New York: Twayne Publishers, Inc., 1964) and Charles S. Holmes's *The Clocks of Columbus* (New York: Atheneum Publishers, 1972).

Books Which Include Discussions of Thurber

Eastman, Max. *The Enjoyment of Laughter*. New York: Simon and Schuster, Inc., 1936.

Ford, Corey. *The Time of Laughter*. Boston: Little, Brown and Company, 1967.

Kramer, Dale. *Ross and The New Yorker*. New York: Doubleday & Company, Inc., 1952.

Nugent, Elliott. *Events Leading Up to the Comedy*. New York: Trident Press, 1965.

Van Doren, Mark. *The Autobiography of Mark Van Doren*. New York: Harcourt, Brace and Company, 1958.

Interviews

"Mr. Thurber Observes a Serene Birthday." Interview with Harvey Breit. *New York Times Magazine*, December 4, 1949, p. 17.

"James Thurber in Conversation with Alistair Cooke." *The Atlantic*, CXCVIII (August, 1956), 36–40.

"Everybody Is Getting Serious." Interview with Henry Brandon. *The New Republic*, CXXXVIII (May 26, 1958), 11–16. Reprinted and expanded as "The Tulle and Taffeta Rut," in Brandon's *As We Are*. Garden City: Doubleday & Company, Inc., 1961.

"Frankly Speaking." Interview with Stephen Potter, B.B.C. Home Service Program, December 24, 1958.

Essays and Selections

Benêt, Stephen and Rosemary. "Thurber—As Unmistakable as a Kangaroo." *The New York Times Book Review,* December 29, 1940, p. 6.

Brady, Charles. "What Thurber Saw." *The Commonweal,* LXXV (December 8, 1961), 274–76.

Connolly, Cyril. "New Fiction." *The Daily Telegraph,* November 26, 1935.

Downing, Francis. "Thurber." *The Commonweal,* XLII (March 9, 1945), 519.

Edman, Irwin. "The Haunting, King-Size Exasperations and Wit of James Thurber." New York *Herald Tribune Book Review,* November 1, 1953, p. 1.

Friedrich, Otto. "James Thurber: a Critical Study." *Discovery,* No. 5 (January, 1955), pp. 158–92.

Gannett, Lewis. "James Thurber: 'Pre-Intentionalist.'" New York *Herald Tribune Book Review,* November 12, 1961, p. 5.

"A Hamlet Who Sometimes Played the Fool." *The Guardian,* obituary essay, November 2, 1961, p. 5.

Holmes, Charles S. "James Thurber and the Art of Fantasy," *The Yale Review,* LV (Autumn, 1965), 15–33.

Mikes, George. "James Thurber," in his *Eight Humorists.* London: A. Wingate, 1954, pp. 107–25.

MacLean, Kenneth. "James Thurber—a Portrait of the Dog Artist." *Acta Victoriana,* LXVIII (Spring, 1944), 5–6.

Moynihan, Julian. "No Nonsense." *The New Statesman,* LXIV (December 14, 1962), 782.

Norton, Dan. "Mr. Thurber's Merry-Go-Round," *The New York Times Book Review,* February 4, 1945, pp. 1, 18.

Prescott, Orville. "Books of the Times" (review of *The Thurber Album*). *The New York Times,* May 28, 1952, p. 27.

"Priceless Gift of Laughter." *Time,* LVIII (July 9, 1951), 88–90.

"The Reeves and the Grotches." *Time,* XLV (February 12, 1945), 45.

"Salute to Thurber." *The Saturday Review,* XLIV (November 25, 1961), 14–18.

"Thurber and His Humor . . . Up with the Chuckle, Down with the Yuk." *Newsweek,* LI (February 4, 1957), 52–56.

Tracy, Honor. "The Claw of the Sea-Puss." *The Listener,* XLVII (May 10, 1951), pp. 760–61.

"Two Institutions." *The Times Literary Supplement,* April 9, 1949, p. 231.

Wilson, Edmund. "Books" (review of *The White Deer*). *The New Yorker,* XXI (October 27, 1945), 91.